C000225738

THE
LITTLE
BOOK
OF
SNOOKER

COMPILED BY SEAN BORU
FOREWORD BY JIMMY WHITE MBE

The History Press

First published 2010

The History Press
The Mill, Brimscombe Port
Stroud, Gloucestershire, GL5 2QG
www.thehistorypress.co.uk

British Library Cataloguing in Publication Data.
A catalogue record for this book is available from the British Library.

ISBN 978 0 7524 5561 7
Typesetting and origination by The History Press
Printed in Great Britain

ACKNOWLEDGEMENTS

We would like to thank Ronnie Wood, Steve Davis, Ronnie O'Sullivan, Ken Doherty and the many other professional players who helped in the making of this book. Without them spending time to talk to us and conveying their great stories and stats, it wouldn't have been as interesting, entertaining and factual as it has turned out.

A special thank you also goes out to World Snooker, without the team at W.S. the players and fans wouldn't be so well-informed about what is happening within this great sport.

World Snooker is a great way to keep up with events on the snooker and billiards scene. It is available at:

www.worldsnooker.com

AUTHOR'S NOTE

In 1998, after forty-six years of good health, I was diagnosed with Hodgkins Lymphoma which came as tumours in my neck. I was cured by Radiotherapy, but it came back again in 2000. I was again given Radiotherapy for a tumour behind the globe of my right eye. In 2002 I found three large and aggressive tumours under my shoulder blade, in my lung and in my spleen. This time I was given Chemotherapy and that seems to have done the trick as the cancer has been dormant since. During the second cancer, I looked for a video to help me understand visually what it was all about. I hated the leaflets and booklets as they were full of jargon. What I needed was a video I could watch that explained it simply. There were videos out there, but they too were full of doctors explaining it in third party terms so, being the way I am, I made my own video, now a DVD. The idea was to film all my Radiotherapy and Chemo treatments with me presenting the film, and speaking from the heart as a patient as I went through it. It was all filmed live and I showed the most intimate bits, positive and negative, to show people, from the viewpoint of a patient, that it isn't all doom and gloom. Where there was gloom, I explain how I felt and why I think I felt that way. I always had the intention of giving the film away for free, and so after completing it that's what I started to do. However, money is tight and I now only give them away when requested. I want to give every cancer patient and their family this film, and I want to help them to understand the wheres and what-fors of it all from the patient's view. It has helped a lot of people and been endorsed as a great aid to patients by many people. Those people include doctors, nurses, consultants, celebrities, patients and families.

I am therefore donating all the royalties from this book to go to provide cancer hospitals and clinics in the UK and Ireland with copies to give away free to patients as soon as they are diagnosed. If you want to assist in providing extra copies for a hospital near you, then email me at seanboru@hotmail.com and I will let you know the company details for ordering them. They will come direct to you, and you can donate them to the hospital with my compliments. I have struck a deal that makes each complete DVD cost just 20p. There is a space on the back of every insert where, if you want to, you can have your details, or your company details recorded as the sponsor. During 2010 I will be at many sporting matches raising more funds to donate more films. For a preview of the film go to http://www.youtube.com/watch?v=0sLXfcLvSH8. It is an 8-minute promo. Thank you for buying this book and helping your fellow man. I hope you are never in need of the film yourself. I will be publishing my updated biography in 2010/11, my website is updated every month and a diary of events will be available for you to see where I will be. I hope you will come along and meet me, and support some of the stars who are supporting this film as well. The website is www.seanboru.com. Now let's get snookering!

Sean Boru, 2010

FOREWORD

I started playing snooker and billiards when I was big enough to reach the table. My dad Tom was on the committee of the social club where I started my career. When I was 14 Alex Higgins came to the club to play an exhibition match, and my love of the sport grew every minute that Alex was at the table. I played him that day, and we have been friends ever since. Snooker has become my livelihood, and I still enjoy playing and promoting the sport every day. It is a challenging sport that has both a physical and a mental side to it, and of course a great deal of patience when your opponent is milking a good run. Like so many other sports there is always the entertainment value of a great frame, especially when your opponent is just as skilled and entertaining. Being able to take the edge off the pressure of a frame, with a little bit of aimed humour, is also something that I and a lot of players appreciate.

I've been very blessed in my snooker career and I've enjoyed the travelling as well – snooker has taken to me many countries that I might never otherwise have visited. Some years ago, myself and a few other players, along with Chas and Dave, even made a record and appeared on *Top of the Pops*, how cool is that! It was called 'Snooker Loopy' and we all said at the time that the title summed up our love for the game. I've also been blessed with the privilege of playing and becoming friends with some awesome players. Steve Davis, Alex, Ronnie O'Sullivan,

John Virgo, Ray Reardon and many more have remained great friends over the years. Today I am now privileged to say I am also friends with many of the younger and upcoming players, like Matthew Stevens for instance. That is the magic of this sport.

Up until the early 1960s, snooker was considered to be a gentleman's sport, in that I mean a sport for the gentry and army officers. Then Alex Higgins came along and opened up the professional sport to all and sundry. I am proud of my achievements and the fact that I'm in a sport that I can play until I'm 90 and still enjoy. Boxers, footballers and athletes don't have that privilege, and I for one am grateful that I do.

I fully support any efforts that promote this wonderful sport, and this book by Sean Boru is a superb example of how to do just that. I've known Sean a few years now and I always enjoy his writing. This book is full of great sportsmen, their achievements, facts about the game, wonderful anecdotes and an enthralling list of historic facts that even I didn't know.

I would like to thank you for keeping the sport alive and supporting it. As a reader and a fan you are the very person that players like me play the game for. I hope you will continue to support the sport, keep going to see the matches and exhibitions and pass on your love to the next generation. Who knows, you may even be the next Higgins, O'Sullivan or White yourself, or they may be your children. Enjoy the facts and the anecdotes and keep the faith.

Jimmy White MBE, 2010

A HISTORY OF THE GAME

A game similar to croquet and 'Pallo à Maglio' was first played in royal palaces and parks as early as 1430 in the reign of King Henry VI. It was played using a billiard club and a ball on a manicured lawn. From this game billiards was developed in the form of 'Pool Games'. Billiards as a name is, it is suggested, derived from the French word 'Billart' which was a mace-style weapon, from which the design of the billiard club emerged. This club was a 3ft stick with a chain at the bottom attached to a metal ball; the player swung the chain and ball to hit the balls on the lawn and potted them into holes. The Chinese warlords also had a similar game as far back as the ninth century although they used balls made from stone and jade.

There is a lot of speculation about the origins of billiards as nothing of any value is documented until around the middle of the seventeenth century. Probably the most authentic and detailed account is *The Compleat Gamester* by Charles Cotton, published in 1674. According to Cotton, billiards was a class sport played throughout Europe, and it was most popular in England where many of the larger towns had public tables, mainly in gentlemen's clubs and gambling houses. Cotton drew an illustration showing an oblong table with six pockets – it was much the same as modern tables, albeit slightly smaller in size.

Around the beginning of the eighteenth century billiards was quite different to our modern game. It was played with only two balls which were then pushed along the table by a cue called a 'Mace' or 'Mast'. The game changed a lot in that century and by 1710 the balls were improved to effect a better flow. Balls were by then made from ivory and replaced the unpredictable wooden balls. An ivory arch, called the 'Port' was positioned on the table where, today, we place the rack. An ivory peg called the 'King' was then placed on another spot at the far end of the table. The rules were to pot your opponent's ball while keeping your own ball out of the pocket. The pocket in this version of the game was called a 'Hazard' and was an obstacle you had to avoid. Points were gained by passing the ball through the 'Port' or hitting the 'King'. A full game was five frames played by daylight or three frames by candlelight. Originally it was played on a smooth wooden board. The cloth covering of tables started in about 1650. In 1734, Cotton's fifth edition book of the game said that the 'Port' and 'King' had been taken out of play, and he mentions cues for the first time.

A 1775 publication of the rules of billiards was called *Hoyle's Games*. This book tells of the introduction of a red ball in a new version of the game which had quickly become popular in parts of Europe. This version Hoyle referred to as 'Caram' which was often also referred to as 'Carambole'. The red ball was the 'Carom', and was in affect the origin of the cannon ball. This version had the red placed on what is now the 'Pyramid Spot'. The players had to shoot from the baulk spot, and you weren't allowed to play back into the baulk, as in the present rules. Both the white and red ball had to be re-spotted after they were potted, but the rules stated that each player only had the one shot, so making a break wasn't possible. The introduction of the red ball according to Hoyle came from the French; they are also accredited with the design of a table with six pockets. The French then changed the rules again and took out the pockets, and what they were left with was the cannon game which was popular in the nineteenth century.

Billiards as we know the game today was, as stated, developed in Europe before coming to England in the early nineteenth century. It was also especially popular in Germany where they played three versions of the game. With the development of the sport came new designs and sizes of table; by the time it became popular in England it was an expensive sport to support and was therefore played only by gentlemen and the aristocracy, and on tables which now had sides and pockets to catch the balls.

In India during the early days of the Raj, the army usually had a billiards table in the officers' mess. The rules were in place by the mid-nineteenth century and the game even had a governing body. One day in 1875 at the officers' mess in Jubbulpore, a new version of billiards was introduced by a Colonel Sir Neville Chamberlain. He simply added more coloured balls to make the game more challenging and to allow more players. Later on that year when a young officer was playing him at the new game, the officer missed a simple shot and was called a 'snooker'. A 'snooker' in the British army was a new recruit and one that would make a lot of mistakes in his early career. From this incident the word spread to all the other army posts, and the new sport soon became known as 'Snooker'.

The first rules of snooker were written and implemented in 1882 at the army headquarters in Ootacamund, India

– the Billiards Association didn't recognise the rules until 1900. They realised that the game of snooker was now as popular as billiards, and decided to welcome the new sport into the association. There are more snippets of how the game developed throughout the book.

DID YOU KNOW THAT . . . ?

A snooker cue cannot be less than 3ft in length, but there is no maximum length. The most common wood used is ash, which is often intertwined with hardwoods. Most players design and balance their own cues which are unique to them.

HE SAID WHAT?

I've had enough of snooker, I'm off mate!
Ronnie O'Sullivan walking out of a frame against Stephen Hendry

BRITISH WORLD CHAMPIONSHIPS

The first official British World Snooker Championship took place at Camkins Hall in Birmingham in 1927 and was organised by the Billiards Association and Control Council. It was won by Joe Davis who beat fellow Englishman Tom Dennis 20–11. The prize money was £10 10s; the highest break was 60 by Albert Cope. Joe went on to win his first Billiards World Championship in 1928, along with his second Snooker World Championship that same year.

Scottish player Walter Davidson was the second world champion in 1947; he beat Fred Davis (brother of Joe) in the final 82–63.

The third world snooker champion was Fred Davis – he ironically beat Walter Davidson 82–63 in 1948. Then in the following year he again beat Davidson, 80–65.

In 1952 the first foreign player won the Billiards Association and Control Council (BACC) title – he was Australian Horace Lindrum and he beat New Zealander Clark McConarchy 94–47. They were the only two entrants. It was given the title of the BA and CC championship title – the last time the title was used.

In 1952 the professional players held an alternative world championship title tournament. It came about after a dispute with the official association, the BACC. The tournament was called the World Matchplay, and the winner was Fred Davis who beat his old adversary Walter Davidson 38–35. This tournament was regarded by the players, the media and the fans as the official World Championship.

MR BROWN? OH YEAH . . . HE'S ALL WHITE! THE QUOTES OF JIMMY BROWN NÉE WHITE

With a bit of luck, the name Jimmy Brown will be engraved on the Masters trophy at the end of next week.

The atmosphere's great but I didn't get the practice I would do at home.

After being distracted by The Crucible atmosphere

I have not come to Sheffield to look at the gardens near the hotel. If I didn't think I could win the World Championship I would go and play golf badly in Spain.

Steve was fantastic in the UK Championship and if he'd played the same game in the final as he had the rest of the tournament I think he would have won it.

I think I've got more chance of winning the Masters now (2006), than I had when I won it in 1984.

I love playing at Wembley. It's the only tournament in London and the only one-table event. I can't wait to get out there.

'NOW I'M SEEING RED,' SAID THE CANNON!

The red ball became popular in the English version of billiards shortly before the start of the nineteenth century. By about 1815 the three-ball game version had overtaken the original game in England and was called the 'Common Game of Billiards'. According to the new English rules, pocketing the opponent's ball was referred to as a 'winning hazard'. If a player lost points by pocketing his own ball, it was called a 'losing hazard'. These rules revolutionised the popularity of billiards and the interest it created helped to develop it into another version that was the opposite to the winning game, where only losing hazards and cannons counted as points. A rule now said that a player could follow a point-winning shot with another one, and so breaks were now part of the rules. The old and the new versions combined in the 1820s to become the modern game. It was known throughout most of the nineteenth century as the 'winning and losing game'. The 1820s popularity of billiards also encouraged the development of the sport in America. Initially it was along similar lines to the English game. The Americans devised their own version of the cannon game using four balls. The four-ball version of the game was extremely popular in America in the nineteenth century.

THE BRITISH OPEN

Final Frame Results (ranking event)

2003	Stephen Hendry	9–6	Ronnie O'Sullivan
2002	Paul Hunter	9–4	Ian McCulloch
2001	John Higgins	9–6	Graeme Dott
2000	Peter Ebdon	9–6	Jimmy White
1999	Stephen Hendry	9–5	Peter Ebdon
1999	Fergal O'Brien	9–7	Anthony Hamilton (autumn)
1998	John Higgins	9–8	Stephen Hendry
1997	Mark J. Williams	9–2	Stephen Hendry
1996	Nigel Bond	9–8	John Higgins
1995	John Higgins	9–6	Ronnie O'Sullivan

1994	Ronnie O'Sullivan	9–4	James Wattana
1993	Steve Davis	10–2	James Wattana
1992	Jimmy White	10–7	James Wattana
1991	Stephen Hendry	10–9	Gary Wilkinson
1990	Bob Chaperon	10–8	Alex Higgins
1989	Tony Meo	13–6	Dean Reynolds
1988	Stephen Hendry	13–2	Mike Hallett
1987	Jimmy White	13–9	Neal Foulds
1986	Steve Davis	12–7	Willie Thorne
1985	Silvino Francisco	12–9	Kirk Stevens

ALEXANDER GORDON HIGGINS: A BRIEF BIOGRAPHY

Alex Higgins very nearly never made it as a snooker player. Although he was said by his school teacher, Mr Walsh, to have had 'a misspent youth playing snooker rather than attending school,' Alex first became interested in becoming a jockey. After school he left his native Belfast for England and spent a few years at the stables of trainer Eddie Reavey in Oxfordshire, during which time Alex was nearly trampled to death by a horse he was exercising. He still managed to keep up his snooker playing though, and later on went to London where he earned a living hustling in the West End snooker halls. On his return to Belfast, Alex joined a league at the YMCA and the rest, as they say, is history.

The Second World War was barely over when Alex blew into the world on 18 March 1949 – no doubt his scream was the loudest the hospital had ever heard.

Alex excelled at his sport and won many titles as an amateur, both as an individual player and as a league team player for boys' clubs. By 1968 he was such an awesome player that he won the All-Ireland Amateur Title and the Northern Ireland Amateur Champion title, just months apart.

He grew up in a tough part of Belfast called Sandy Row, and ironically now lives back there in a new block of flats. The club where Alex started playing snooker at the age of nine is long gone, but Alex and his incredible career have made the name of the Jampot Club a legend around the world. He was always supported by his mam and dad and his three loyal sisters in his early career.

Today Alex is a legend among modern day greats such as Jimmy White and Ronnie O'Sullivan. It was Alex's playing in the 1982 World Championship that inspired a six-year-old Ronnie to take up the cue, while Jimmy met Alex in his dad's social club at age fourteen when Alex came to play an exhibition and Jimmy played him a frame. Jimmy and Alex have been great mates since then, and today the pair still thrill the fans as they play exhibition matches in Ireland and the UK to packed clubs and halls.

First turning professional in 1971 at the age of twenty-two, he made a name for himself on the exhibition circuit as well as the competition circuit. However, just a year later he took Sheffield by storm and won the World Championship on his first attempt.

Alex was always a controversial player, and is accredited with bringing snooker 'kicking and screaming' into the twentieth century. He is said to have made a

£3m-plus fortune out of the sport, but then spent it on the good life. He was married twice, first to Cara Hasler in Australia in April 1975, and then to Lynn Avison in England in January 1980. He has two children from his marriage to Lynn: Jordan and Lauren.

When he won the 1982 World Championship, he then invited Lynn and Lauren down to the table. He cried with joy at having won the title for Lauren as he had promised her he would do so. That particular championship at Sheffield was also a sad one for Alex as, in order to get into the final, he had to beat his old mate Jimmy White in the semi-final. Alex never got over winning that title at the expense of Jimmy, although Jimmy always says 'it was just part and parcel of what we do as sportsmen, there is never anything personal in beating a friend at snooker and taking a title.'

Always controversial, Alex had a long-running argument with the old WPBSA on various issues, numerous court hearings never seeming to settle the issues. Alex was in trouble with the association on more than one occasion, usually ending in a ban or a fine, but it never lost him any fans.

There is no match played by Alex that is considered the 'best one' – they are all thought of as masterpieces of his incredible ability to pot a ball with speed and agility. However, his big downfall has always been his inconsistency of play; he can be a master of the baize in frame after frame, then suddenly lose his edge and, subsequently, the match.

He never learned to drive a car, although he has owned several in his time.

In June 1998 Alex's world was 'turned upside down' when he went to a Manchester hospital for tests on his sore throat and later learned he had cancer. He was so down about it at first that he thought he was going to be breathing his last very soon. He returned to Belfast and was treated in the general hospital; he recovered after many sessions of Radiotherapy and his confidence quickly returned.

Alex had a portrait painted of himself which once hung in the Belfast art museum, but after they closed for a long refurbishment, the painting failed to reappear and is thought be in storage in the basement.

All in all Alexander Gordon Higgins, aka 'the Hurricane', has been responsible for making snooker what it was in its heyday and, to an extent, today. He has brought joy to his legions of fans in many countries around the world and is still considered to be the most famous player in the history of the game. There have been many books written about him, some of which Alex says 'are a work of fiction', but his own book, *From the Eye of the Hurricane*, is said by him to be the only true reflection of the real Alex Higgins.

HE SAID WHAT?

He was one of the best-looking snooker players we ever had, and had a heart like a lion.

Willie Thorne on Paul Hunter

TERRENCE GRIFFITHS OBE:
A BRIEF BIOGRAPHY

These days Terry is running his own academy, and works closely with World Snooker to promote etiquette and skill in the game. Being born in Llanelli in Wales on 16 October 1947, Terry was almost destined to follow family traditions and work as a coal miner. His dad was a member of the local social club and they had a snooker table where a young Terry used to be fascinated as he sat with dad and his uncles on a Saturday morning watching the players.

It was when he was around nine or ten that Terry managed to get players to give him some tips and even some lessons and games. From that first shot, a champion was obviously born, and Terry spent much of his spare time playing on that table. This wasn't a case of a misspent youth in a smoky snooker hall, missing school and gambling for pocket money; Terry was a meticulous student and even in his teens had his heart set on a career other than as a sportsman. He was good enough to be accepted into the social club team, and played as an amateur in local and national leagues. He soon came to notice, and by sixteen he was ready to take on the best of the local players in the Llanelli and District championships. It was a hard play for him, but he persevered and won the Llanelli and District Amateur League championship in 1963. He knew then that he had a potential career as a professional should he choose to go down that road. He went on to be a better player every season, albeit still as an amateur. He worked as a bus conductor, an insurance salesman and a policeman during the years he was building up his game. His best amateur season came in 1975 when he went on to win the Welsh Amateur title. Shortly afterwards, being the entrepreneur he was, he personally organised an exhibition match against Alex Higgins. Having Higgins on a bill was a sure-fire way of selling tickets. The event soon sold out. The local community was rooting for 'their boy', and even the local brewery got involved when they offered to sponsor the after party. The match was held in the community hall and, despite all his skill and experience, Alex fell foul of the local boy and was beaten that night. This was the inspiration Terry needed, and he decided shortly afterwards to cast his net wider and enter the English Amateur Championship, which he won in 1977, and followed it up by taking the title again the following year.

Terry had a long talk with his boss and his family who all supported his thoughts on turning professional – after all he had won several amateur titles and had beaten some of the best professionals in exhibitions! He was thirty-one and just starting out in his new career as a professional sportsman. He thought it was ironic that many sportsmen were at the peak of their career at this age. His new professional career didn't start well, though – he was beaten in his first pro match, but only just, and this in no way deterred him. He spent the best part of his first year just playing and getting adjusted to the gruelling travelling; little did he realise that all this new experience was about to catapult him to stardom. His first big win came just a year after turning pro and it was the top prize in snooker; Terry could not have known when he walked through the hallowed doors of the Sheffield Crucible in 1979 that he would emerge a few weeks later as the new World Champion. To just reach the quarter-finals would have been enough at his first ever attempt. He again beat Alex Higgins as well as other well-established players to win a place in the semi-finals against Eddie Charlton who had no intention of letting this new upstart get the better of him. Eddie gave Terry a hard set of frames and made him work for his supper; Terry must have been just happy enough to get that far and played some superb snooker in his stride. It was close, but Terry won the match and ended up in the final against Dennis Taylor. The press were frantic to get the low-down on this new challenger, and in one interview with the BBC he made the audience laugh when he exclaimed 'I'm in the final, you know!' It seemed to everyone that it had suddenly dawned on him how well he had done. That was the interview that won Terry so many new fans – here was not only a great champion in the making, but a nice guy to boot. The next day he took Dennis Taylor to task and eventually won 24–16 to a tumultuous cheer from The Crucible crowd, his family, his mates from Llanelli and millions of fans at home.

Terry has always been a proud Welshman. He's never forgotten his roots or the debt he always felt he owed his fellow countrymen for their faith and encouragement. He was very pleased to be part of the Welsh team along with other snooker greats such as Ray Reardon and Doug Mountjoy. Indeed, shortly after winning the World Championship he was part of the winning Welsh team who beat England 14–3 in the final, and there seemed to be no end to his winning formula. He did lose out to

John Virgo in the final of the UK Championships though, but it didn't seem to make any difference to him. He was determined that a few months later on he would become the first player to return to Sheffield and retain the title, breaking the infamous 'Crucible Curse' that decreed all returning champions would be out of the competition fairly early. After Christmas Terry started practising with more vigour than ever; he went on to beat Alex Higgins, again, to take the Benson & Hedges Masters title in a spectacular final score of 9–5. It was his first Masters and the Griffiths luck was certainly helping his incredible play.

Before he went back to Sheffield to defend his title, he popped across the Irish Sea to scoop the Benson & Hedges Irish Masters, again at his first attempt. However, the match took its toll on him and he only just took the title with a final score of 9–8 against his Welsh team-mate Doug Mountjoy. At The Crucible, Terry was confident of retaining his title. He remembers seeing an up-and-coming player walk into the theatre on day one, a red-headed young man named Steve Davis. It was Steve who knocked Terry out of the competition in the second round, smashing his hopes of taking the title again and beating the curse.

He was still hugely popular on the exhibition circuit, and entered all the remaining major competitions in 1980. His play and his luck fluctuated; he was part of the winning Welsh team again in the World Championships, and he again won the Irish Masters, but he went out early in the UK Masters and never won the title again. Over the next two years he found himself constantly up against Steve Davis in most of the finals he managed to get to. Davis beat him in all but two of them.

By 1982 Terry was settled into his place in snooker history, he was a competitive player and still winning titles and setting new records for consistency. In the Lada Classic that year Steve Davis performed a televised 147, but it was Terry Griffiths who walked away with the title. He again won the Irish Masters that year, becoming the first consecutive treble winner. He went out in the first round at Sheffield, and that seemed to be the final death knell on him winning titles. His last major UK title win was the UK Masters later that year, where he beat old adversary Alex Higgins in a nail-biting 16–15 final. He never won any more UK ranking titles, but made up for that by winning many international titles, mainly in the Far East.

By the early 1990s Terry began to struggle in the rankings, although he still managed to reach the semi-final of the 1992 World Snooker Championship, but lost his place in the final to Stephen Hendry. When he lost at The Crucible in 1996 to Steve Davis, he immediately announced his retirement from snooker. Terry did, however, play at The Crucible one last time in 1997, but lost 10–9 to fellow Welshman Mark Williams in a final-frame decider. He is noted as having played a total of 999 frames at The Crucible.

He is hailed by everyone in snooker as one of the most consistent, polite and worthy champions in snooker history. He now spends his time coaching and encouraging new players and is also an ambassador for not only snooker and World Snooker, but also for his home country of Wales.

WHEN THE LEFT HAND KNOWS WHAT THE RIGHT IS DOING!

Ronnie O'Sullivan has an extraordinary ability to play with both hands. The first time he did it at a tournament was in the 1996 World Championship against Alain Robidoux. Canadian Robidoux accused him of disrespect and said that Ronnie was insulting his play by doing it. An astonished Ronnie replied that he played better with his left hand than Robidoux could with his right. Robidoux was having none of it after Ronnie knocked him out of the competition, so he made an official complaint to the WPBSA. Ronnie was summoned to a disciplinary hearing and protested his innocence. He was asked to prove that he could play to a high level with his left hand, by playing against board member Rex Williams. He played three frames of snooker against the former world championship runner-up – and won all three. The charge of bringing the game into disrepute was subsequently dropped.

HE SAID WHAT?

A lot of snooker players are too intense and serious, I want to be more like Billy the Kid.

Ronnie O'Sullivan

THE SCOTTISH OPEN AND INTERNATIONAL

From 1981 up to 1997 the tournament was known as an international tournament. Then it changed to the Scottish Open.

The Scottish International Open

1981	Steve Davis	9–0	Dennis Taylor
1982	Tony Knowles	9–6	David Taylor
1983	Steve Davis	9–4	Cliff Thorburn
1984	Steve Davis	9–2	Tony Knowles
1985	Cliff Thorburn	12–10	Jimmy White
1986	Neal Foulds	12–9	Cliff Thorburn
1987	Steve Davis	12–5	Cliff Thorburn
1988	Steve Davis	12–6	Jimmy White
1989	Steve Davis	9–4	Stephen Hendry
1993	Stephen Hendry	10–6	Steve Davis
1994	John Parrott	9–5	James Wattana
1995	John Higgins	9–5	Steve Davis
1996	John Higgins	9–3	Rod Lawler
1997	Stephen Hendry	9–1	Tony Drago

The Scottish Open

1998	Ronnie O'Sullivan	9–5	John Higgins
1999	Stephen Hendry	9–1	Graeme Dott
2000	Ronnie O'Sullivan	9–1	Mark J. Williams
2001	Peter Ebdon	9–7	Ken Doherty
2002	Stephen Lee	9–2	David Gray
2003	David Gray	9–7	Mark Selby

PLAYER OF THE YEAR AWARD

Each year the Snooker Writers' Association makes an award for the player of the year, here are the winners:

Steve Davis	1983, 1984, 1986, 1987, 1988, 1989
Joe Johnson	1986 (jointly with Steve Davis)
Stephen Hendry	1990, 1991, 1992, 1993, 1995, 1996, 1997
Ronnie O'Sullivan	1994, 2001, 2004, 2005, 2008
Dennis Taylor	1985
Paul Hunter	1998
John Higgins	1999, 2006, 2009
Mark J. Williams	2000, 2003
Peter Ebdon	2002
Neil Robertson	2007

WHO WANTS TO BE A MILLIONAIRE?

The top ranking money-earners in prize money (approx):

Stephen Hendry	£8,790,000
Ronnie O'Sullivan	£6,730,000
Steve Davis	£5,550,000
Jimmy White	£4,710,000
John Higgins	£4,680,000
Peter Ebdon	£2,546,000
Alan McManus	£2,340,000
Dennis Taylor	£1,565,000

James Wattana	£1,540,000
Matthew Stevens	£1,525,000
Paul Hunter	£1,510,000
Stephen Lee	£1,490,000
Terry Griffiths	£1,475,000
Neal Foulds	£1,330,000
Willie Thorne	£1,310,000

HE SAID WHAT?

If snooker hadn't existed, TV would surely have had to invent it.

Geoffrey Nicholson

WORLD CHAMPIONS SINCE 1969

John Spencer:	1969, 1971 and 1977
Ray Reardon:	1970, 1973, 1974, 1975, 1976, 1978
Terry Griffiths:	1979
Cliff Thorburn:	1980
Alex Higgins:	1972, 1982
Joe Johnson:	1986
Steve Davis:	1981, 1983, 1984, 1987, 1988, 1989
John Parrott:	1991
Ken Doherty:	1997
Stephen Hendry:	1990, 1992, 1993, 1994, 1995, 1996, 1999

Mark J. Williams:	2000, 2003
Peter Ebdon:	2002
Ronnie O'Sullivan:	2001, 2004, 2008
Shaun Murphy:	2005
Graeme Dott:	2006
John Higgins:	1998, 2007

DINNER'S OVER, LET'S CLEAR THE TABLE!

By 1810, billiard tables were made with a solid wooden bed. The most popular were made from good old reliable English Oak, roughly 25mm in thickness and, because of the weight, it was cut and planed in three equal slices. Some tables still in existence show that marble and parquet beds were also made. These wooden-bedded tables were a lot lighter than today's examples. Furniture makers often made them a dual-purpose table – they had a solid table top cover to allow it to double up as a dining table. This came about because billiard tables at that time were mostly made by furniture craftsmen and they sensibly made them this way to make them popular with the lady of the house.

The cushions were stuffed with a variety of materials. To keep costs down many makers used a material known as 'list' which is a waste product that comes from the process of making cotton into a workable product. The bigger makers used horse hair which was plentiful before the advent of the motor car, while some used cheap felt cut-offs, another waste product from the hat-making industry. However, the use of all these materials produced a hard padded surround, which tended to slow up the ball when it hit the sides. Being inventive, the players started developing ways to turn this disadvantage into an advantage. One of the newly developed shots was the 'Jenny Shot' into the middle pocket which could easily be repeated almost every time and became a popular move.

HE SAID WHAT?

Whoever called snooker 'chess with balls' was quite rude, but right.

Clive James

JUST LIKE A ROLLIN' STONE: CELEBRITY FANS

Rolling Stones guitarist Ronnie Wood always has a snooker room at his house and he is a fanatical player, albeit an amateur one. The Rolling Stones usually have a table on tour with them – it is how they all like to chill out before and after a gig.

Ronnie is best mates with snooker legend Jimmy White. The pair met at a school play in which both their daughters were performing. When Jimmy was busy filming the cast prior to the play, Ronnie spotted him and walked over. With his video camera in his hand, he raised it up and then said to Jimmy, 'are you as good with that camera as you are with a cue?' Jimmy didn't cotton on at first and slyly looked at the man to his left. Seeing it was Ronnie Wood he just replied, 'are you as good with that camera as you are with a guitar?' The pair then fell about laughing as Ronnie admitted that he didn't know one end of the camera from the other. They went for a drink afterwards and have been really good friends ever since. Whenever the pair have a day free they often meet up, and just spend the day playing, and no doubt drinking a little as well. Jimmy often gets a call inviting him to Ronnie's home to play a few frames with other legends of the game, and vice versa. Even though they now live miles apart, they still meet up quite a lot and Ronnie apparently spent a fortune voting for Jimmy when the 'Whirlwind' was in the jungle in 2009, on *I'm a Celebrity, Get Me Out of Here.*

Ronnie has said that his biggest break to date is 42, and no matter how many times he plays with the champions, he still can't seem to improve on that. He has been described as 'having a nice style, perfect cue action, but hits the ball too hard.' Rock legends, eh! When Jimmy came up against Ronnie O'Sullivan in a semi-final at Wembley, Ronnie was there watching the play. He later recalled ' it was a case of 'déjà vu' for me.' Ronnie Wood was reflecting on one particular night when both the players happened to be at his St John's Wood house together. He continued, 'Whenever Ronnie [O'Sullivan] and Jimmy come over to visit they liked to play a grudge match. If they miss a ball, they rack up and start the frame all over again. This particular night they were a bit the worse for wear due to some vodka, and so kept on playing until the sun came up, which put me right in the doghouse with Jo. However, I didn't really mind that much – it is always a pleasure to be in the company of such great players as these two.'

HE SAID WHAT?

I think it's a great idea if you talk during sex, just so long as it's about snooker.

Steve (not so boring after all) Davis

GRAND PRIX FINAL FRAME RESULTS

The Professional Players' Tournament

1982	Ray Reardon	10–5	Jimmy White
1983	Tony Knowles	9–8	Joe Johnson

The Grand Prix

1984	Dennis Taylor	10–2	Cliff Thorburn
1985	Steve Davis	10–9	Dennis Taylor
1986	Jimmy White	10–6	Rex Williams
1987	Stephen Hendry	10–7	Dennis Taylor
1988	Steve Davis	10–6	Alex Higgins
1989	Steve Davis	10–0	Dean Reynolds
1990	Stephen Hendry	10–5	Nigel Bond
1991	Stephen Hendry	10–6	Steve Davis
1992	Jimmy White	10–9	Ken Doherty
1993	Peter Ebdon	9–6	Ken Doherty
1994	John Higgins	9–6	Dave Harold
1995	Stephen Hendry	9–5	John Higgins
1996	Mark J. Williams	9–5	Euan Henderson
1997	Dominic Dale	9–6	John Higgins
1998	Stephen Lee	9–2	Marco Fu

| 1999 | John Higgins | 9–8 | Mark J. Williams |
| 2000 | Mark J. Williams | 9–5 | Ronnie O'Sullivan |

KEN DOHERTY:
A BRIEF BIOGRAPHY

Ken Doherty was born in Dublin on 17 September 1969. He became interested in snooker after watching Alex Higgins win the final of the World Championships in 1982. He used to practice at a local snooker hall called Jason's in his native Ranelagh – he won the world championship using a cue he bought from the snooker hall for €2.

Ken became only the third player from outside the United Kingdom to win the World Championship after beating Stephen Hendry 18–12 in the 1997 final. Ken also reached the World Championship final in 1998, losing to John Higgins and in 2003, losing narrowly to Mark Williams. That championship got Ken noticed for some impressive comebacks, including a final-frame win over Shaun Murphy, and a semi-final comeback from 9–15 to beat Paul Hunter 17–16. In that championship he played more frames than anyone before or since.

The World Championship of 2005 saw Ken beat Barry Pinches in the first round 10–5. Although he won the last 8 frames, he was knocked out in the second round by Alan McManus 13–11.

Following an average start to the 2005 season, Ken won the Malta Cup in 2006. He beat John Higgins with a magnificent display of sportsmanship in the final. Ken had been trailing 8–5 at one stage, but he managed a stirring comeback, winning four frames in a row. He later told a press conference that he considered the victory to be his 'most important tournament win since the World Championship.'

In the 2006 World Championship, Ken started well, winning his first match and defeating Barry Hawkins 10–1. He followed that up by beating Matthew Stevens, again playing some brilliant snooker to win the last five frames. He was the bookies' favourite in the quarter-final match against Marco Fu, but lost 13–10. The final session started at an even 8–8, but Ken struggled through the rest of the frames. He did, however, battle back to win a frame in which he required three snookers. Ken led 7–6, 8–7, 9–8 and 10–9, but could never quite take that two-frame advantage that could have given him the fortitude to win the match. At a press interview he said, 'I blew it big time, but I still have a couple more years to win the title.'

Ken made a good start to the 2007 season by reaching the quarter-final of the Northern Ireland Trophy at Waterfront Hall in Belfast. Ken's game is a tactical one and he often feels he doesn't always score heavily enough, although he is also capable of making big breaks and has done so on many occasions. His careful and cautious approach has led to the nickname 'Crafty Ken'. In 2000 he narrowly failed to achieve a maximum 147 break when he missed a relatively easy final black off its spot in the 15th frame of the Benson & Hedges Masters final against Matthew Stevens. To date, Ken has compiled around 248 centuries in competition during his career. He used to practise in Jason's of Ranelagh, Dublin, where he learned to play handicap snooker tournaments on Saturday mornings. Jason's closed in 2006 and now Ken practices in his own private room in a hotel in Dublin. He started playing in national tournaments from the age of sixteen after getting sponsorship from Jason's. In his first national event, an Under-16 ranking tournament, Ken lost the final but he was back a month later to beat the man who had beaten him in the Irish Under-16 National Championships.

Ken still lives in Ranelagh Village, Dublin, and is married to Sarah, an Australian psychiatrist. He was nearly blinded in 2002 in a bathroom accident. He slipped on the wet floor and his face struck an ornament, the blow narrowly missing his left eye. That distinctive scar on his right cheek goes back to his seventh birthday, when he fell off a shed roof on to a metal dustbin.

Recently, he started working on TV studio coverage of snooker matches with the BBC snooker team, along with his old mates Steve Davis and John Parrott. Ken is a huge Manchester United fan and he paraded his trophy at Old Trafford in front of 55,000 spectators following his World Championship triumph.

HE SAID WHAT?

The time is right for more good companies to get on board the snooker train, and if that happens then the game will be very big again, as it was in the 1980s.

Shaun Murphy

'OIL' BE THERE TO STRIKE A LIGHT, GUV!

Lighting on a table is something that today we find necessary, but in the days before the discovery of electricity and the popularity of indoor gas mantles, billiards was mostly played using natural light. Unlike our modern day snooker halls which rarely have windows, early games were played in rooms that deliberately had lots of glazing. It was also popular to play outside in the summer and on warm days in the winter. In the 1860s lanterns were introduced indoors, these hung over the tables, but were not really useful as they tended to cast shadows. They were run using cabbage seed oil which burned brighter than conventional oils, it was called Colza.

DID YOU KNOW THAT . . . ?

The modern form of snooker chalk is not actually chalk but a compound of silica and corundum. It was invented by snooker player William Spinks with the help of a chemist friend in 1897.

UK CHAMPIONSHIPS

1977	Patsy Fagan	12–9	Doug Mountjoy
1978	Doug Mountjoy	15–9	David Taylor
1979	John Virgo	14–13	Terry Griffiths
1980	Steve Davis	16–6	Alex Higgins

1981	Steve Davis	16–3	Terry Griffiths
1982	Terry Griffiths	16–15	Alex Higgins
1983	Alex Higgins	16–15	Steve Davis
1984	Steve Davis	16–8	Alex Higgins
1985	Steve Davis	16–14	Willie Thorne
1986	Steve Davis	16–7	Neal Foulds
1987	Steve Davis	16–14	Jimmy White
1988	Doug Mountjoy	16–12	Stephen Hendry
1989	Stephen Hendry	16–12	Steve Davis
1990	Stephen Hendry	16–15	Steve Davis
1991	John Parrott	16–13	Jimmy White
1992	Jimmy White	16–9	John Parrott
1993	Ronnie O'Sullivan	10–6	Stephen Hendry
1994	Stephen Hendry	10–5	Ken Doherty
1995	Stephen Hendry	10–3	Peter Ebdon
1996	Stephen Hendry	10–9	John Higgins
1997	Ronnie O'Sullivan	10–6	Stephen Hendry
1998	John Higgins	10–6	Matthew Stevens
1999	Mark J. Williams	10–8	Matthew Stevens
2000	John Higgins	10–4	Mark J. Williams
2001	Ronnie O'Sullivan	10–1	Ken Doherty
2002	Mark J. Williams	10–9	Ken Doherty
2003	Matthew Stevens	10–8	Stephen Hendry
2004	Stephen Maguire	10–1	David Gray
2005	Ding Junhui	10–6	Steve Davis
2006	Peter Ebdon	10–6	Stephen Hendry
2007	Ronnie O'Sullivan	10–2	Stephen Maguire
2008	Shaun Murphy	10–9	Marco Fu
2009	Ding Junhui	10–8	John Higgins

THE DARK THOUGHTS OF
RAY 'DRACULA' REARDON

Ronnie O Sullivan is the most naturally gifted player the game of snooker has ever seen.

I cannot remember anyone ever asking, 'Who came second?' Can you?

HE SAID WHAT?

The physical and mental pain of playing snooker has been taking its toll on me recently, I may consider quitting.

Ronnie O'Sullivan

CLOSE THAT CHAMPIONSHIP!
DON'T YOU KNOW THERE'S A WAR ON!

During the Second World War no championship tournaments were played. This was partly because many of the professionals were serving in the forces. It was considered that to hold the tournament would be unfair competition. Joe Davis held the title without any challenge from 1941–5. When the tournament resumed in 1946 Joe again won the title which he had held consistently from 1927.

From 1958–63 no tournaments were held, owing to a lack of sponsors as the game had declined in popularity.

From 1964–8 it was known as the World Championship and decided by challenge matches.

From 1969 to the present the World Championship is decided by knockout matches.

GO WITH THE FLOW MO, IT'S A WINNING MOVE!

Billiard table baize in the early nineteenth century was made from a coarse commercial grade that was used to make working clothing. The spots were made by hammering brass tacks into the wooden bed. This crude type of table covering wasn't very good, and a player had to get used to the way the table cambered in order to be good. Gambling on games was popular too, and you had an advantage as a punter if you knew that a particular player 'knew the table'.

NORTHERN IRELAND TROPHY FINAL FRAMES

2005	Matthew Stevens	9–7	Stephen Hendry
2006	Ding Junhui	9–6	Ronnie O'Sullivan
2007	Stephen Maguire	9–5	Fergal O'Brien
2008	Ronnie O'Sullivan	9–3	Dave Harold

OOH! YOU'RE SO STREAKY

Snooker is considered to be a gentleman's sport, but that hasn't stopped it being victim to the dreaded 'sports streaker'. Every snooker player who ever held a cue in competition fears the streaker. Most people will remember Erica Roe who famously streaked at that now infamous Twickenham rugby match, but few remember the brave men and women who have bared their all, literally, for the Good Ship Snooker and all who sail in her. Most do it for a bet, some do it for the publicity and a few have been known to do it just for the hell of it. The first was Lianne Crofts who made an appearance to remember in the final of the 1997 Benson & Hedges Masters. The frame was between Steve Davis and Ronnie 'The Rocket in my Pocket' O'Sullivan (OK, so I made that bit that up!). Steve however, managed to keep his cool thoughout the whole ordeal, and won the match 10–8. Soon afterwards the trend took off, along with the clothes, with two streakers at the World Snooker Championship. First off with his clobber was Andrew Slater – to hide his modesty he wore a Sven-Göran Eriksson mask and matching socks. It happened during a 2002 match between Quinten Hann and Paul Hunter.

The next naked runner made an appearance at the 2004 final between Ronnie O'Sullivan and Graeme Dott. This time the 'birthday suit' boy was Mark Roberts, who ran down the stairs then tried to hide his modesty, and everything else, under the table. Ronnie was in fits of laughter and made some comments that had the crowd clapping and cheering. There must be something about Ronnie 'Rocket' O'Sullivan that makes people strip off and run around in public, for during the 2008 final between Ronnie and Ali Carter, Mark Roberts made a comeback appearance. Mark ran across the arena and again dived under the table. Ronnie was about to get up from his chair to take his first ball, if you'll excuse the pun! Ronnie later remarked that he felt he was being 'stalked', which in his native Essex means something else entirely.

HE SAID WHAT?

In time, snooker will pay a fitting tribute to Paul Hunter. I don't think anything will do his loss justice, but I'm sure there will be something special for him to be remembered by.

Michael Holt

UK MASTERS FINAL FRAMES

1975	John Spencer	9–8	Ray Reardon
1976	Ray Reardon	7–3	Graham Miles
1977	Doug Mountjoy	7–6	Ray Reardon
1978	Alex Higgins	7–5	Cliff Thorburn
1979	Perrie Mans	8–4	Alex Higgins
1980	Terry Griffiths	9–5	Alex Higgins
1981	Alex Higgins	9–6	Terry Griffiths
1982	Steve Davis	9–5	Terry Griffiths
1983	Cliff Thorburn	9–7	Ray Reardon
1984	Jimmy White	9–5	Terry Griffiths
1985	Cliff Thorburn	9–6	Doug Mountjoy
1986	Cliff Thorburn	9–5	Jimmy White
1987	Dennis Taylor	9–8	Alex Higgins

1988	Steve Davis	9–0	Mike Hallett
1989	Stephen Hendry	9–6	John Parrott
1990	Stephen Hendry	9–4	John Parrott
1991	Stephen Hendry	9–8	Mike Hallett
1992	Stephen Hendry	9–4	John Parrott
1993	Stephen Hendry	9–5	James Wattana
1994	Alan McManus	9–8	Stephen Hendry
1995	Ronnie O'Sullivan	9–3	John Higgins
1996	Stephen Hendry	10–5	Ronnie O'Sullivan
1997	Steve Davis	10–8	Ronnie O'Sullivan
1998	Mark J. Williams	10–9	Stephen Hendry
1999	John Higgins	10–8	Ken Doherty
2000	Matthew Stevens	10–8	Ken Doherty
2001	Paul Hunter	10–9	Fergal O'Brien
2002	Paul Hunter	10–9	Mark J. Williams
2003	Mark J. Williams	10–4	Stephen Hendry
2004	Paul Hunter	10–9	Ronnie O'Sullivan
2005	Ronnie O'Sullivan	10–3	John Higgins
2006	John Higgins	10–9	Ronnie O'Sullivan
2007	Ronnie O'Sullivan	10–3	Ding Junhui
2008	Mark Selby	10–3	Stephen Lee
2009	Ronnie O'Sullivan	10–8	Mark Selby

WORLD RECORD 147s

The first report of a professional player making the maximum break of 147 was that of E.J. Murt O'Donoghue of New Zealand, at Griffiths in New South Wales, Australia, on 26 September 1934.

Leo Levitt became the first amateur to achieve a maximum break, in November 1948 at the Winsor Bowling alley in Montreal, Canada.

The first officially declared 147 in an exhibition match, was by Joe Davis at the Leicester Square Hall, London, on 22 January 1955.

The first 147 in a major tournament was by John Spencer at Slough in Berkshire on 13 January 1979, but the table had oversized pockets.

Steve Davis had a ratified break of 147 when he played John Spencer in the Lada Classic at Oldham on 11 January 1982. This was also the first televised maximum.

Cliff Thorburn was the first player to make two tournament 147 breaks on 23 April 1983 and on 8 March 1989. This was also the first double 147 break in the World Professional Championships. Peter Ebdon and James Wattana have also achieved this feat.

Ronnie O'Sullivan made a 147 break when he was 15 years and 98 days old, during the English Amateur Championship at Aldershot on 13 March 1991.

The youngest player to score a 147 break in a competition was Judd Trump – he was 14 years and 206 days old. It was in an under-16 series match against Chris Piech at the Potters Club in Coalville on 13 March 2004.

Stephen Hendry became the first player to make more than two tournament 147s. The first was during the European League and his second was during the 1995 World Championship. His record-breaking third came on 25 November 1995 in the UK Championship. Stephen then made his fourth maximum on 5 January 1997 in the Liverpool Victoria Charity Challenge. Then he made his fifth on 23 May 1998 in the Dr Martens Premier League. Stephen wasn't going to let anyone steal his record and on 19 September 1999, in the final of the British Open, he scored his sixth 147 break which was also the first maximum in a ranking final. Stephen then made his seventh maximum in November of 1999 in the Liverpool Victoria UK Championship. His eighth maximum break came on 25 February 2001 in the final of the 2001 Rothmans Grand Prix!

Ronnie O'Sullivan and Stephen Hendry jointly hold the record for the highest amount of maximums with nine. Ronnie's ninth came at the 2008 888.com World Championship; it was during the last frame of his second-round match against Mark J. Williams. Stephen's ninth came on 28 April 2009 in the quarter-finals of the 2009 Betfred.com World Championship.

Ronnie O'Sullivan and Jimmy White both made 147 breaks in consecutive frames during an exhibition in Ireland in January 2009.

'IVORY' A BETTER BALL THAN YOU MATE!

By the beginning of the nineteenth century ivory balls had already been in use for over a hundred years, and were the most common balls used for English championship matches. These were made from African ivory which was thought to be denser than its Indian cousin. A consistent density was necessary to maintain a set of equally playable balls – if the density was inconsistent then the balls all ran at different rates of speed. This consistency was considered so significant that the balls were weighed before the start of all important matches. Although the size of each ball might differentiate slightly, the weight was the most important factor in selecting a matching set of balls. A tusk is just like a tooth, and the elephant tusk has a nerve running through its centre just as a tooth does. This results in a hole that is quite big in balls that are cut from the base of a tusk. So, when making balls, manufacturers used the smaller tusks of the cow elephant, which are usually much denser with a smaller nerve hole. Holes created by the nerve would usually be plugged with ebony and become the 'spot'. Another problem was that ivory is porous which means that a ball can change its shape during a game owing to the absorption of moisture, especially in a humid room or outdoors. It was common for players to carefully place their ball so that the top and bottom of the nerve hole were as horizontal as possible.

HE SAID WHAT?

I don't like Shaun Murphy, and I think the feeling is mutual.

Stephen Maguire

I CAN BEAT THAT: BREAKS HIGHER THAN 147

It is possible to achieve a 16-red ball clearance break that is in excess of a score of 147.

The highest snooker break in competition is Wally West's 151. He made the break in the final of a club handicap at the Lucania Club in Hounslow in 1976. It happened during the second frame when opponent Derek Rogers clipped the blue, and left Wally snookered. Wally potted the green as his free ball and then potted the brown to follow. He then took 14 red and blacks and a pink off the last red to achieve the score of 151.

In 1976 Alex Higgins knocked in a 146 when he played Willie Thorne in a Challenge Match. He had brown, green, 10 blacks and 5 pinks.

Steve Duggan made a witnessed break of 148 in a practice frame with Mark Rowing in Doncaster, South Yorkshire, on 27 April 1988.

Stephen Hendry made a 148 in a practice match with Alfie Burden in 1993.

In 1995 Tony Drago recorded a 149 in a practice match against Nick Manning at the West Norwood Snooker Club. Tony broke off and snookered Nick behind the brown. Nick tried to escape from the snooker, but left a free ball. Tony took the brown as his free ball and then the brown again for four more points, He followed that with 15 reds, 13 blacks, a pink, a blue and then all the colours.

Eddie Manning also achieved a 149 in 1997 at Willie Thorne's club in Leicester. His practice partner was Kam Pandya. Eddie took brown, and then brown again, then 13 blacks, a pink and a blue.

On 23 April 2003, seventeen-year-old Jamie Cope made a 151 break on the match table at the Reardon Snooker Club during a practise game with David Fomm-Ward. After a foul shot by his opponent, Jamie was snookered behind the brown ball. He took the brown as his free ball then potted the blue, 8 reds and 8 blacks, 2 reds and 2 pinks, 5 reds and 5 blacks. He then cleared all the colours.

In 2006, now a professional snooker player, Jamie Cope became the first player to record a 155 break. He did it in a witnessed practice match.

Jamie Burnett made a break of 148 on 16 October 2004 at the Prestatyn qualifiers for the Travis Perkins UK Championship. This was the first break over 147 in professional snooker. Jamie made the break in the 14th frame of his match against Leo Fernandez. He potted the brown as the extra red, then another brown followed by the 15 reds and all the colours. He made a blue on the first red, a pink on the last one and another pink on one of the other reds. The rest went with blacks. He won the match 9–8.

WELSH OPEN FINAL FRAME RESULTS

1992	Stephen Hendry	9–3	Darren Morgan
1993	Ken Doherty	9–7	Alan McManus
1994	Steve Davis	9–6	Alan McManus
1995	Steve Davis	9–3	John Higgins
1996	Mark J. Williams	9–3	John Parrott
1997	Stephen Hendry	9–2	Mark King
1998	Paul Hunter	9–5	John Higgins
1999	Mark J. Williams	9–8	Stephen Hendry
2000	John Higgins	9–8	Stephen Lee
2001	Ken Doherty	9–2	Paul Hunter
2002	Paul Hunter	9–7	Ken Doherty
2003	Stephen Hendry	9–5	Mark J. Williams
2004	Ronnie O'Sullivan	9–8	Steve Davis
2005	Ronnie O'Sullivan	9–8	Stephen Hendry
2006	Stephen Lee	9–4	Shaun Murphy
2007	Neil Robertson	9–8	Andrew Higginson
2008	Mark Selby	9–8	Ronnie O'Sullivan
2009	Ali Carter	9–5	Joe Swail
2010	John Higgins	9–4	Ali Carter

28p AN HOUR . . . I'M NO JOB'S WORTH!

Steve Davis has only ever had three jobs in his life. Before and after leaving school he worked in a butcher's shop, but soon gave that job the 'chop' when he realised he was never going to have a 'steak' in the business. He then progressed in life to a job in a greengrocer's shop. He wasn't as 'cabbage-like' as he looked though, for his wages dramatically increased from 28p an hour to around £1,000 an hour, when he finally took that giant leap for snooker-kind, and turned professional. Since then he has been the 'apple' of every snooker fan's eye!

HE SAID WHAT?

If Ronnie O'Sullivan or anyone else thinks snooker on ice, or played in sequinned outfits is the way forward, I'd be happy to listen to the their proposals.
Sir Rodney Walker, former Chairman of World Snooker

THE CURIOUS CASE OF THE NEW CUE

The cue as a tool in billiards and snooker took a long time to be developed. It eventually replaced the old mace in the billiard rooms of France, Italy and Germany, and then it travelled to England. It all came about when the continentals started to turn the mace around – instead of using the 'thick end', they started using the 'thin end'. It was so much easier to strike a ball that lay on the cushion using this method, and it just sort of stuck! This led to individual and specifically designed cues, with some being developed just for a particular kind of shot. They had a plain thick wooden end which was squared off with a special cut. The other end was honed to a taper, which was much better for striking the centre of a ball with more directional control. Most billiard clubs and gambling houses only allowed the best players to use the new style cues – it was more for safety than snobbery though, as it was common for new inexperienced players to rip the cloth with the new style cue.

Another first in enabling players to strike parts of the cue ball other than the centre, was by the design of the 'Jeffrey Cue'. This was cut obliquely at the point enabling a player to strike the ball just below the centre.

Next came a cue with a slightly rounded tip which helped to prevent a miscue if the player was slightly offset with his centre ball-striking.

The leather tip of the cue was invented by a French cavalry officer, Capt. Mingaud, in about 1807 when he was on remand in prison due to his outbursts of political views when drunk. However, American William Lake, a billiard-playing cobbler, also claimed the invention at about the same time. The inventor isn't important though; what is important is that this simple ingenious idea brought a much-needed evolution to the modern game, and more so than any other single factor.

THERE'S NO BUSINESS LIKE . . . WELL . . . MONKEY BUSINESS!

Fred Davis was playing a match at the Spectrum Arena in Warrington in 1985. As Fred entered the building he was greeted by a mix of pandemonium and giggling. Intrigued as to what was going on, he walked straight into the main arena to see what all the fuss was about. Four security men and a number of officials were busy trying to catch a chimpanzee which had escaped from a nearby circus. The cheeky monkey had made his way to the Spectrum and sneaked inside. By now a group of spectators had gathered in the seated area and were watching the attempted capture with some delight. One member of the public caught sight of Fred and asked him what he thought of it all. Being the Northern wit that Fred was he simply asked, 'is this my opponent?' The man laughingly replied that he didn't think it was, to which Fred replied back, 'Well, there are so many new professionals these days, I don't know half of them.'

THE IRISH MASTERS

This event was the biggest tournament in Ireland and was very well attended by the fans, and the best players. It ran from 1978 to 2005.

1978	John Spencer	5–3	Doug Mountjoy
1979	Doug Mountjoy	6–5	Ray Reardon
1980	Terry Griffiths	9–8	Doug Mountjoy

1981	Terry Griffiths	9–7	Ray Reardon
1982	Terry Griffiths	9–5	Steve Davis
1983	Steve Davis	9–2	Ray Reardon
1984	Steve Davis	9–1	Terry Griffiths
1985	Jimmy White	9–5	Alex Higgins
1986	Jimmy White	9–5	Willie Thorne
1987	Steve Davis	9–1	Willie Thorne
1988	Steve Davis	9–4	Neal Foulds
1989	Alex Higgins	9–8	Stephen Hendry
1990	Steve Davis	9–4	Dennis Taylor
1991	Steve Davis	9–5	John Parrott
1992	Stephen Hendry	9–6	Ken Doherty
1993	Steve Davis	9–4	Alan McManus
1994	Steve Davis	9–8	Alan McManus
1995	Peter Ebdon	9–8	Stephen Hendry
1996	Darren Morgan	9–8	Steve Davis
1997	Stephen Hendry	9–8	Darren Morgan
1998	Ken Doherty (Ken lost to Ronnie O'Sullivan, but Ronnie was stripped of the title after failing a drugs test)		
1999	Stephen Hendry	9–8	Stephen Lee
2000	John Higgins	9–4	Stephen Hendry
2001	Ronnie O'Sullivan	9–8	Stephen Hendry
2002	John Higgins	10–3	Peter Ebdon
2003	Ronnie O'Sullivan	10–9	John Higgins
2004	Peter Ebdon	10–7	Mark King
2005	Ronnie O'Sullivan	10–8	Matthew Stevens

MARY QUEEN OF SHOTS!

Mary Queen of Scots was imprisoned for an attempted coup against Queen Elizabeth I. Her prison was Fotheringhay Castle, and as a concession she was allowed a billiard table in her room. It was quite common for women to play the game as it needed little physical effort and, even with all their stays and corsets on, they could still beat the men. Just before her execution the table was confiscated and she complained of this to the Archbishop of Glasgow. She is rumoured to have then made a bizarre request that her body be wrapped in the baize, which apparently was granted.

DICKIE BIRD:
ANOTHER CELEBRITY FAN!

Legendary cricket umpire Dickie Bird can often be spotted sitting in the audience at The Crucible when the World Snooker Championships are on. It would appear that he loves snooker as much as some of the snooker players love cricket. His birthday happens to be on 19 April, around the time that the championships are on – he has said on many occasions that it is just a birthday treat.

Since retiring from cricket umpiring he pursues his love of other sports, and can name many a non-cricket sporting legend among his friends. Born in 1933, Dickie has followed snooker and billiards for most of his adult life, so he is quite a respected expert on the game and the players, old and new. He is an honoured guest in the

Green Room, and can often be found deep in conversation with the usual snooker commentators. Cricket umpiring aside, he would have loved to have been a professional snooker player. He has no preferred favourites, or at least he's not admitting to any! He loves the company of Willie Thorne, Steve Davis, John Virgo and Dennis Taylor as they are regular commentators, and when Dickie is in for the day he loves to get all the week's gossip over a pot or two of tea.

His biggest break is in the 50s and he has never managed 100 to date, but he says he lives in hope. He actually played snooker in his youth at the YMCA club in Barnsley, South Yorkshire. In those days he was known by his birth name of Harold Bird – the Dickie name is an affectionate play on his surname. He has a great admiration also for the umpires. Being one himself, he appreciates the concentration and skill required.

He received an MBE from the queen in 1986 for his contribution to sport and his charity work. He has now set up the Dickie Bird Foundation, which helps disadvantaged juniors achieve their potential in sport.

BLACK BALL SHOOT-OUTS AT THE K.O. CORRAL

Black ball shoot outs are usually played to decide all out winners in really close finish matches. The black ball is re-spotted, the match is then awarded to the player who pots it in the least amount of shots; here are a few that made the news.

The 1975 Benson & Hedges Masters was decided on a re-spotted black ball; John Spencer potted the black and won the match against Ray Reardon.

Stephen Hendry won an edge-of-your-seat re-spotted black in the 1994 Top Rank Event in Thailand. He was later quoted as saying he was lucky to have been able to leave the country, his opponent having been James Wattana.

In the 1980 World Team Cup, Dene O'Kane played for the Rest of the World with Steve Davis playing for the England side. They were forced to a re-spotted black to decide who would have the privilege of holding the cup aloft. Davis, who was the England Captain, defended his reputation for being cool under fire and potted the final black.

EUROPEAN OPEN FINAL FRAME RESULTS

1989	John Parrott	9–8	Terry Griffiths
1990	John Parrott	10–6	Stephen Hendry
1991	Tony Jones	9–7	Mark Johnston-Alan
1992	Jimmy White	9–3	Mark Johnston-Alan
1993	Steve Davis	10–4	Stephen Hendry (1992/3 season)
1993	Stephen Hendry	9–5	Ronnie O'Sullivan (1993/4 season)
1994	Stephen Hendry	9–3	John Parrott
1996	John Parrott	9–7	Peter Ebdon
1997	John Higgins	9–5	John Parrott
2001	Stephen Hendry	9–2	Joe Perry
2003	Ronnie O'Sullivan	9–6	Stephen Hendry
2004	Stephen Maguire	9–3	Jimmy White

HE SAID WHAT?

Hugh Grant is just a geezer and a great laugh, although he is a bit corrupting. But he did get me interested in golf, cricket and snooker.

Nicholas Hoult

MARIE ANTOINETTE – 'LET THEM PLAY BILLIARDS'

In France where the game was most popular in the eighteenth century, the royal and aristocratic women were actually better at billiards than the men. When the people of France began to revolt in Paris in 1789, Marie Antoinette was playing a frame with her ladies-in-waiting, and when the news reached the Palace of Versailles she is alleged to have said of their plight, 'If they are hungry and there is no bread, let them eat cake.' Instead of defying the masses, she would have been well advised to have challenged their leaders to a game of billiards – chances are she would have wiped the floor with them. Every class of citizen in France played the game by the time Marie was eventually executed. Unlike her royal connection Mary Queen of Scots, during her incarceration Marie Antoinette was not allowed to indulge in the playing of a game of billiards. Maybe her guards were frightened that she would actually beat them! She died of a severed head on 16 October 1793, an ardent fan and player of the game.

HE SAID WHAT?

If I had to make the choice between staying married and playing snooker, snooker would probably win every time. Don't tell the wife though, will you!

Ray Reardon

CUE UP NOW LADS, HERE'S A GOOD TIP!

Long before the design of the leather tip, chalk was known to have been popular among the more fanatical players (it was a handy tool to have in preventing miscues). When the chalked tip was first used, the effects of applying 'side' to a cue ball became appreciated by most players. In 1828 Thurston's started making coloured chalk in blue; before that the colour was white.

It is generally believed that the two-piece cue is a relatively modern invention, but as far back as 1829 the two-piece was made and sold by Thurston's. Also in about 1830, new cues, which had previously been made from a single piece of ash, became popular with a spliced decorative design at the butt. This style quickly became fashionable among players in the trendy London clubs. They were made of heavier woods although Thurston's also manufactured an ash cue with a bamboo butt from 1832.

At the same time designer cue cases were being sold. They were made from polished mahogany and designed to hold two or more cues. Cues were also now starting to be made to order for individual players.

The word 'cue' comes from the shape – when it was used the other way around the thinner end was similar to a tail, which the French called a 'Queue'.

HE SAID WHAT?

I don't know if I'm still the 'Rocket', perhaps I'm more like Thomas the Tank Engine these days!

Ronnie O'Sullivan

SCOTTISH MASTERS FINAL FRAMES

Lang's Scottish Masters:

1981	Jimmy White	9–4	Cliff Thorburn
1982	Steve Davis	9–4	Alex Higgins
1983	Steve Davis	9–6	Tony Knowles
1984	Steve Davis	9–4	Jimmy White
1985	Cliff Thorburn	9–7	Willie Thorne
1986	Cliff Thorburn	9–8	Alex Higgins
1987	Joe Johnson	9–7	Terry Griffiths

Regal Scottish Masters:

1989	Stephen Hendry	10–1	Terry Griffiths
1990	Stephen Hendry	10–6	Terry Griffiths

1991	Mike Hallett	9–6	Steve Davis
1992	Neal Foulds	10–8	Gary Wilkinson
1993	Ken Doherty	10–9	Alan McManus
1994	Ken Doherty	9–7	Stephen Hendry
1995	Stephen Hendry	9–5	Peter Ebdon
1996	Peter Ebdon	9–6	Alan McManus
1997	Nigel Bond	9–8	Alan McManus
1998	Ronnie O'Sullivan	9–7	John Higgins
1999	Matthew Stevens	9–7	John Higgins
2000	Ronnie O'Sullivan	9–6	Stephen Hendry
2001	John Higgins	9–6	Ronnie O'Sullivan
2002	Ronnie O'Sullivan	9–4	John Higgins

STEVE DAVIS OBE:
A BRIEF BIOGRAPHY

Steve Davis was born on 22 August 1957 in Plumstead, London. He started playing as a competitive amateur at the age of twelve. He would travel from his South London home to the Lucania snooker club in Romford, Essex. His skills were soon recognised by the amateur Essex champion Vic Harris – he in turn spoke highly of Steve to the chairman of the club, Barry Hearn. By the time he was twenty-one in 1978, he was already a big name on the snooker circuit with many titles for billiards and snooker behind him. In that same year he made his professional debut at the World Snooker Championships although he was knocked out in the first round 11–13 by Dennis Taylor.

Not one for being perturbed by defeat, Steve brushed himself down and got going the following year. He was again knocked out of the 1980 World Championship, but not until the losing in a quarter-final to Alex Higgins. Later on that year he won the 1980 UK Championship, this time beating Alex Higgins 16–6 in a brilliant final. In 1981 he had his wish granted and became the world champion after a brilliant series of matches against the best players on the circuit. He beat Doug Mountjoy 18–12 to establish himself as the new kid on the block.

Steve then went on to win another five world championships in just eight years, along with a string of other titles to go with the trophies he proudly keeps on show at his mansion in Brentwood, Essex. He has won in excess of £5.5m in prize money during his illustrious career.

In January 1982 Steve made snooker history by making the first televised 147 break. Then, in 1988, Steve was awarded an MBE for his contribution to British sport and was also voted BBC Television Sports Personality of the Year. In 2001 he was again honoured, this time with an OBE, and it is greatly predicted that he will one day be given a knighthood.

On top of his achievements in the sporting world of snooker and billiards, Steve has also won respect for his poker playing skills. He is a regular player on the poker circuit along with fellow snooker ace Jimmy White and actor Michael Greco, all of whom have won some money in competition. The three friends play regular games at the Royal Surrey Snooker Club in Morden, which is owned by Jimmy White.

Steve is also an accomplished radio personality as well as a sporting pundit on TV. He has DJ'd on Essex

Radio and Phoenix FM and his favourite music is soul music.

Chess is another sport that Steve has mastered and he has been a president of the British Chess Foundation. Also, in 2000, he won the World Pool Championship which is another sport he is involved in. Steve Davis is also the president of the Snooker Writers' Association which has many members, from professional players to snooker coaches and members of the writing fraternity. They aim to keep the sport in the public eye by writing articles about the players, tournaments and the sport in general.

Contrary to his reputation as a boring man, Steve Davis is in fact a very humorous personality. The nickname Steve 'not very interesting' Davis came about as part of a lampooning of him on the TV show *Spitting Image*. Steve saw the funny side and in fact he used it to further his off-the-table career. He has made a DVD and appeared in a number of hilarious adverts where he uses the nickname to promote products, including one for baked beans that had a snooker slant to it.

HE SAID WHAT?

Playing snooker gives you firm hands and helps to build up character – which makes it the ideal recreation for dedicated nuns.

Luigi Barbarito

DID YOU KNOW THAT . . . ?

The Players Championship Trophy was only played once. That was in 2004, and Jimmy White won the trophy after beating Paul Hunter 9–7 in the final. The tournament started life in 1981 as the Jameson International, then it was renamed the International, then the Matchroom Trophy. It was mostly known as the Scottish Open thereafter until 2003.

OOH! VIRGO; I NEVER KNEW YOU CARED!

While commenting on a match, John Virgo said:
John Parrott wants a screw . . . with plenty of bottom.

THE GREAT HAUL OF CHINA

The British Champs
China loves snooker, mainly because it is a sport they can bet on. The Chinese therefore have some very lucrative competitions in which the world's best players perform alongside some of the best of the new kids on the block. In China it is not unusual to find a snooker table in the middle of a park or a busy market. The British players continue to dominate the Chinese competitions. The results of two of China's best-known competitions are:

The Honghe Industrial China Open
Held at the Beijing University, the prize purse is £250,000.

1999	John Higgins	9–3	Billy Snaddon
1999	Ronnie O'Sullivan	9–2	Stephen Lee
2000	Ronnie O'Sullivan	9–3	Mark J. Williams
2002	Mark J. Williams	9–8	Anthony Hamilton
2005	Ding Junhui	9–5	Stephen Hendry
2006	Mark J. Williams	9–8	John Higgins
2007	Graeme Dott	9–5	Jamie Cope
2008	Stephen Maguire	10–9	Shaun Murphy
2009	Peter Ebdon	10–8	John Higgins

The Shanghai Take Away!
The Shanghai Masters is China's second championship; instituted in 2007 it has again been dominated by the British players.

2007	Dominic Dale	10–6	Ryan Day
2008	Ricky Walden	10–8	Ronnie O'Sullivan
2009	Ronnie O'Sullivan	10–5	Liang Wenbo

IT'S TOO HARD DEAR; LET'S GET A NEW BED!

The first design of table that had a rubber cushion bed was quite unique. They were made up from L-shaped pieces of wood with an overhang. The idea was that the ball would hit the cushion around its middle, then deflect evenly back down the table. The design came about to solve the problem of bouncing balls, which tended to hurtle in all directions around the table. This method of using the overhang basically gave the player some control on the angle of the deflection. In the English game the cushions were simply an addition, rather than a new design. Using a material that didn't include any natural rubber sap, Thurston's tables converted a table at the officers' mess of the 42nd Hussars in Corfu in May 1835. However, Thurston's didn't invent the concept of rubber cushions – that was the idea of Belgian billiards table manufacturers who had been using the concept for some years previously. The most common problem with natural rubber was that the cold made the cushions hard, and this made it necessary to warm them up before and during a match. Thurston's new sides solved that problem to some extent, although many tables still had the old style, natural rubber sides. In 1838 Thurston's made a present to Queen Victoria and Prince Albert of some specially designed hot water bottles to soften the sides – at that time the servants used to remove the sides and warm them up in front of the open fire in the snooker room at Windsor Palace. Some people also used a type of hot iron to heat up the sides, this was done using a device that a blacksmith would insert a white-hot piece of metal into.

DID YOU KNOW THAT . . . ?

Jimmy White's middle name is Warren.

MATTHEW STEVENS, PHILOSOPHER OR NOT?

It was a bit of a scrappy match, apart from the two frames where I made centuries.

I feel as fresh as a daisy now, as if I've not played a game so far in this tournament. I've been going to bed early and getting up early, so far it's paid off. I know that for sure as I have just beaten Jimmy White.

It's my first final for a while. It's been a tough couple of years for me, but I've been working hard at my game. I started in June this season, a couple of months early!

THE CRAZY WORLD OF ALEX HIGGINS

Terry Wogan was interviewing Alex just after he received his ban for head butting a referee at the Crucible.

Terry Wogan: So tell us about the head butt, Alex.
Alex Higgins: That was the world's most expensive head butt. It cost me so much money in fines and lost prize money that I went into recession six months before the country did.

Down on his luck, Alex found himself in London without enough money to get back to Manchester, so when an opportunity arose for a free lift he took it.

Alex was on the phone to a reporter in a London hotel lobby. The reporter was desperate for an interview and so Alex agreed to one, but only if the reporter did the interview in the back of a London black cab while giving Alex a lift to see a girlfriend. The reporter agreed to pick Alex up and take him to where he was going in the cab. The cab pulled up outside the hotel and Alex jumped in and sat down. 'Where to, Alex?' asked the reporter as the driver listened intently for the reply. 'Manchester, and make it quick I'm already an hour late and my dinner's probably in the bin,' replied Alex with his usual wry sense of humour. The reporter reluctantly obliged and swore to never get caught by Alex again.

While ghostwriting the Alex Higgins autobiography, Sean Boru used to like having Alex staying with him at his Dublin flat. One night Alex fancied a drink and so, at about 10 p.m., they walked over the Queens Bridge at Ushers Island, and into the Voodoo Lounge which is owned by Huey Morgan of the band Fun Lovin' Criminals. As they entered the pub, a band could be heard playing loudly in the bar. As they passed the pizza take away which is in the pub's entrance hall, they were stopped by three guys who were seated at a table in front of the door into the bar. 'That will be €5 each please gents,' a big fella said to Alex. Looking down his nose through his glasses, Alex said to him, '€5 for what?' 'For the band,' the big fella replied. 'But I don't want to listen to the band, I only want a drink,' said Alex. With that the guy said, 'It doesn't matter, it's still €5 cover charge.' Alex took a step back and, winking at Sean, he said to the big fella, 'Do you know who I am?' and the big fella says, 'Yes I know who you are Alex and I won't hold that against you, so it's still only €5.' With that Alex smiled at him, and the big fella melted at the Higgins charm as Alex puts his hand up to the fella's cheek. 'Ah! Go on then . . . and don't be listening to the music as you're drinking,' the big fella said as he waved them in. Always one for having the last word, Alex turned to the big fella as he passed him and said, 'Don't worry, babe, I won't . . . you see I'm a music lover!'

CHAMPIONS CUP FINAL FINAL FRAMES

Liverpool Victoria Champions Cup:

1999	Stephen Hendry	7–5	Mark J. Williams

Champions Cup:

2000	Ronnie O'Sullivan	7–5	Mark J. Williams
2001	John Higgins	7–4	Mark J. Williams

BY GEORGE, HE'S ONLY GONE AND WON IT!

George Washington was a huge fan of billiards. In 1750, at the age of eighteen, he played the local champion in a town called Alexandria, Virginia. Washington was working in the area as a surveyor at the time, and used to while away the long, hot nights at the newly established billiard hall. The game had a 'winner take all' pot of $25, which was accumulated from heats played during the evening. The best of nine frames was won easily by young George 6–3. He carried on playing the game right up his death on 14 December 1799 having served as the first President of the United States.

WWW.NICKNAMES-R-US.CUE

As all good football teams have a nickname, so do all the professional snooker players. Some however have more than one; here are 20 of them to start with:

Steve Davis	The Nugget, The Ginger Magician, Steve 'Interesting' Davis, Romford Slim
Jimmy White	The Whirlwind
Joe Swail	The Outlaw, The Outlaw Joey Swail
John Parrot	The Entertainer, Mr JP
Mark Selby	The Jester from Leicester
Matthew Stevens	The Welsh Dragon
Nigel Bond	The Basildon Bond, 00-147
Paul Hunter	The Beckham of the Baize, The Man with the Golden Cue
Ken Doherty	Scarface, The Ranelagh Rascal, The Dublin Destroyer, Ken-Do, The Dublin Darling, Crafty Ken The Comeback King
Ronnie O'Sullivan	The Rocket, The Essex Exocet, The Magician, Mr 147
Alex Higgins	The Hurricane, (it should be noted that Alex wanted to be called 'Alexandra the Great', but his management advised against it.)

Tony Drago	The Tornado
Marco Fu	Full of Eastern Promise, Hong Kong Fuey
Dave Harold	The Bloke from Stoke, The Stoke Potter, Banana man, The Hard Man
Quinten Hann	The Wizard of Oz
Ray Reardon	Dracula
James Wattana	The Thai-Phoon
Michael Holt	The Hitman
Mark Allan	Eagle Eye, All in
Mark Williams	The Welsh Potting Machine, Turbo Taffy

HE SAID WHAT?

Mark Selby is playing well enough to get to the final, but I still fancy my chances of going on and winning.

John Higgins

SLATE BEDS VS WOODEN BEDS

Thurston's brought out a new sized ball in 1830 – a 2in billiard ball – which replaced the smaller $1\frac{7}{8}$in ball. By 1833 players were using lead weights placed into holes drilled in the butt of the cue. At that time cues would weigh around 14 or 16 ounces, these were much lighter than modern cues anyway. The extra weight gave the thrust more power, and increased the accuracy of shots. Thurston's started selling slate bed tables en masse in

1835. They had been experimenting with the material for nearly ten years, and could now produce a better quality table for a reasonable price. The slate thickness was between $7/8$in to 1in – about the same thickness as the wooden beds. Slate beds were already popular in Ireland, but they didn't take off in a big way and very few manor houses had them.

THE EUROPEAN CHAMPIONSHIP FINALS

Men's Finals:

1988	Stefan Mazrocis (England)	11–7	Paul Mifsud (Malta)
1993	Neil Mosley (England)	8–6	Robin Hull (Finland)
1994	Danny Lathouwers (Belgium)	8–0	Stefan Van der Borght (Belgium)
1995	David Lilley (England)	8–7	David Gray (England)
1996	Graham Horne (Scotland)	8–5	Kristjan Helgason (Iceland)
1997	Robin Hull (Finland)	7–3	Kristjan Helgason (Iceland)
1998	Kristjan Helgason (Iceland)	7–2	Alex Borg (Malta)
1999	Björn Haneveer (Belgium)	7–0	David Bell (Wales)

Women's Finals:

1996	Kelly Fisher (England)	6–3	Karen Corr (N. Ireland)
1997	Kelly Fisher (England)	5–3	Kim Shaw (England)
1998	Karen Corr (N. Ireland)	5–2	Kelly Fisher (England)
1999	Kelly Fisher (England)	5–2	Wendy Jans (Belgium)

THE GREEDY GETS – SHARE IT AROUND LADS! MULTIPLE CHAMPION TITLE HOLDERS

Joe Davis was world snooker champion for fifteen consecutive years, from 1927–46 (with a break caused by Hitler). Joe also held the Billiards World Champion title for five consecutive years from 1928–32 during this period.

Steve Davis has won a record 28 ranking titles.

Stephen Hendry has outranked Steve Davis with 36 ranking titles to date.

HE SAID WHAT?

Snooker these days has gone right down the tubes. It's being run by friends of friends who couldn't organise a raffle.

Alex Higgins (who else!)

CONSECUTIVE WINNING RECORDS

Kelly Fisher holds the record for the longest winning streak in snooker history. Her winning streak started on 9 June 2001 when she beat Christine Sharp 3–0. It ended on 3 March 2003 after she was defeated 4–3 by Maria Catalano. Kelly won fifteen major women's snooker tournaments and sixty-nine straight matches.

From March 1990 to January 1991, Stephen Hendry won five successive titles and thirty-six consecutive matches in ranking tournaments.

During the summer of 1992, Ronnie O'Sullivan won thirty-eight consecutive matches in qualifying competition.

Stephen Lee (England) won thirty-three frames in a row in the 1992 qualifying competition.

THE TED LOWE SCHOOL OF SILLY QUOTES

'Whispering' Ted Lowe is famous as the quietly spoken commentator and authority on snooker. Ted is also famous for his bloopers. Here are some of our favourites:

For those viewers watching in black and white, the pink ball is just behind the green ball.

And [Terry] Griffiths has looked at that blue four times now, and it still hasn't moved.

Ninety-nine times out of a thousand he would have potted that ball.

He's lucky in one sense, and lucky in the other.

Oh and that's a brilliant shot. The odd thing is his mum's not very keen on snooker.

Higgins first entered the Championship ten years ago. That was for the first time, of course.

And it is my guess that Steve Davis will try to score as many points as he can in this frame.

Steve Davis has a tough consignment in front of him.

A little pale in the face, but then his name is White.

That pot puts the game beyond reproach.
All square, all the way round.

There is I believe, a time limit for playing a shot. But I think it's true to say that nobody knows what that limit is.

Jimmy White has that wonderful gift of being able to point his cue where he is looking.

DID YOU KNOW THAT . . . ?

The first woman referee was Michaela Tabb in 2003.

Michaela was also the first female referee at the world championship final in Sheffield in 2009.

The first ladies World Champion was Vera Selby in 1976. She didn't take up the game until she was thirty-seven!

STEPHEN HENDRY
PHILOSOPHER OR NOT?

People talk about darts being on the crest of a wave. But if that's what we've got to do, let people in drinking and shouting and bawling, then it's a sad state.

The demons are still there. You make your own luck in this game, but if you feel as uncomfortable as I do out there things are not going to happen for you at the right time.

I should have got absolutely rat-arsed on my birthday, but instead I spent the day practising.

I got my good fortune at the start of the match, I fluked a ball and got a lucky snooker but I had enough chances to win three matches.

Things are just not happening for me.

My luck went against me at the wrong time towards the end of the match. That's what happens when you're struggling for results.

If you make loads of unforced errors and miss lots of easy balls, you really don't deserve anything.

I'll stay away from the TV set. I don't give a monkey's who wins it. If I'm out I don't care.

I think snooker is a classy sport, and to go down that route would be a backward step.

Talk that the game is dying is complete nonsense.

STRIKE A LIGHT, GUV!

By 1850 gas lighting was common and many snooker rooms replaced oil lamps with it as a means of playing at night. The countryside was a little behind the towns in getting gas piped into homes, so until the 1890s when that started happening, daylight and oil lamps continued to be the manner of lighting a game. Sky lights were also introduced in the 1850s as a means of eliminating shadow casting, but this could only happen in single-storey rooms or where the snooker room was on the top floor.

STEPHEN HENDRY – CENTURY RECORD HOLDER

Stephen Hendry holds many world records and here are a few more that Stephen has managed to accumulate:

Most centuries in one match:
7 – against Ken Doherty in the 1994 UK Championship final

Most centuries in one event:
16 – in the Embassy World Championship, 2002

Most centuries in one season:
52 – 1995/6 season

Most centuries in professional competition:
726 – up until February 2009

WE'VE BEEN SNOOO-ZZZZZ-KERED!

The longest frame took 93 minutes and 59 seconds to complete. It was between Cliff Thorburn and Stephen O'Connor in 1994.

In 1989 Steve Davis and Dene O'Kane took 73 minutes and 30 seconds to complete a frame.

Mick Price and Chris Small took a yawning 72 minutes and 15 seconds to complete a frame at the 1995 British Open.

HE SAID WHAT?

You can't really call playing snooker a job these days. People often talk about the world rankings and their importance, but how can you judge players on only six tournaments a season? It's not like golf which has about forty events a year.

Matthew Stevens

WAM BAM . . . THANK YOU MA'AM!

The fastest frame on record lasted just 3 minutes and a few seconds. It was between Tony Drago and Danny Fowler in 1988.

The fastest 9-frame match was in 1993. Tony Drago whitewashed Sean Lanigan 5–0 in just 34 minutes.

In 1996 Stephen Hendry beat Jimmy White 6–0 in just 72 minutes and 58 seconds, in the fastest 11-frame round recorded.

HE SAID WHAT?

Ted Lowe, the famous BBC snooker commentator, was remarking on a snooker player (who shall remain anonymous) who was getting on a bit in years, when he made this gaffe:

He can't get his leg over any more. So he's having to rely on using that left hand.

A MATERIAL CHANGE IN THE CLOTH

In the 1850s, baize was a much finer cloth which gave the ball a greater amount of accuracy and travel. Most of the finest cloth baize was produced in the industrious north of England where the Industrial Revolution had brought in mass production of all kinds of cloth material. The spots were by now made from circular pieces of thinly sliced black plaster which were glued to the cloth. They often caused the ball to jump, so they weren't used for professional matches where the position of the spots was marked with compressed chalk powder.

YOU CAN BET YOUR 'HATTON' THAT!

Boxing champion Ricky Hatton grew up around snooker and pool tables; his father was a publican and the family usually lived above the premises. He started playing pool on the pub tables, but Ricky is quite small and his brother Matthew used to get a beer crate for him to stand on. They still play snooker together at their local snooker hall in Hyde, Cheshire.

During training sessions for his fights, Ricky likes to chill out by playing frame after frame. He says he finds it incredibly relaxing to be playing a sport outside of his chosen career. Ken Doherty, Ronnie O'Sullivan and

Jimmy White have all tried to teach Ricky the 'long shot', but he still hasn't managed to master it.

Ricky likes the banter and friendly rivalry that the snooker players have between them. In boxing it is generally used in an aggressive way to get the publicity machines working. 'Some of the more funny comments that are made in snooker just wouldn't work in boxing,' he has said. Controversial players who attract not only the press, but also the fans, are his most watchable players. 'When you look at most sports these days, it is the likes of Alex Higgins and Ronnie O'Sullivan that bring in the fans. In boxing these days we miss the greats such as Muhammad Ali, Joe Frazier and others who were such entertaining ambassadors for the sport outside of the ring. Ronnie and Alex are such publicity makers that no matter what they do or say, the sport of snooker usually wins out of it – it does this by placing bums on seats and that's what it is all about for the people who organise these events.'

Ricky has a fantasy where sports people would indulge in other sports with their fellow rivals, 'For instance, I would love to see some of the snooker players in a boxing match, maybe Jimmy White against Matthew Stevens or how about Alex Higgins against Ray Reardon! Then perhaps I could play a game of snooker against Lennox Lewis, now that would be entertaining.'

HE SAID WHAT?

Every time I play Ronnie I play my best snooker, so this is very special. I hope I can play as well as that again, but it's going to be tough. I may not play as well as that ever again.

Marco Fu on Ronnie O'Sullivan

SOMEONE'S GOTTA BE FIRST!

The world's first recognised world billiards champion was William Cook. He beat John Roberts Snr in the final of the first world championship in 1870. The score was 1,200–1,083. Roberts' son later beat Williams to save the family name. Roberts Jnr and Cook dominated the game for almost 40 years between them.

EVENING ALL, EXCUSE MY DIRTY FACE!

Ray Reardon worked in a coal mine, and was a policeman before turning professional.

ARE YOU THICK OR WHAT?

In about 1870 the thickness of slate beds started to increase when a company named Burroughes & Watts started producing tables with slate beds that were between 1 and 1½ inches thick. These tables had up to four slates per table, but the problem of sagging and noise was still there. Slate beds began to be produced in thicker sections in an attempt to overcome both these problems. High end tables started to have slate sections of 1½ to 2 inches thick. The number of sections also increased to five as a standard for the sport. The increase in weight needed an increase in the number of legs and it wasn't unusual to see eight-legged tables. After a lot of trials and discussions, an agreement was reached on a thickness of 1¾ inches as a standard across the board.

HONG KONG WHITE FUEY . . .

Jimmy White appeared in a Chinese gangster movie. He was persuaded to play the part by the director who was a snooker fan.

BILLY WHIZZ . . . THE FASTEST 147

At The Crucible in 1997 Ronnie O'Sullivan potted a 147 score in 5 minutes and 20 seconds. The frame was against Mick Price and it has yet (2010) to be beaten. The whole display was commentated on by Dennis Taylor, and the crowd gave the 'Rocket' a standing ovation.

OH NO! HOW EMBARRASSING IS THAT?

More gaffes from the commentators who, straight afterwards, had wished for the ground to open up and swallow them:

Steve Davis with his sip of water, which is part of his make-up.

Ted Lowe

He has to stay level or one frame behind, that's the only way he can beat him.

Dennis Taylor

That's inches away from being millimetre perfect.

Ted Lowe

Well it seems at the moment as if the pockets are as big as goal posts for Willie Thorne.

John Pullman

The formalities are now over, and it's down to business; Steve Davis is now adjusting his socks.

Ted Lowe

Well, the shot would have been safe if the red hadn't ended up over that pocket.

Ted Lowe

Steve Davis is trailing by one frame, so the pressure is balanced on him.

Rex Harris

He's obviously worked out for himself that he doesn't need that last red, great thinker this man.

Dennis Taylor

And Jimmy White's potting is literally doing the commentary here.

Ted Lowe

He's completely disappeared. He's gone back to his dressing room, nobody knows where he has gone.

Ted Lowe

THERE'S NO 'ARM IN IT . . . REALLY!

An Irish snooker player who never turned professional, is famous on the circuit because he plays despite only having one arm. Tommy McCarthy, who now lives in Kildare, was a friend to many professional players during the peak of snooker fever in the 1970s and '80s. His family moved to London in the 1950s where Tommy grew up in Enfield. At the age of sixteen a motorbike accident put paid to his dream of becoming a snooker professional as he lost his left arm. However, Tom wasn't one to be put off his dreams so he did the next best thing. He worked hard and eventually opened his own snooker club in Wexford, Ireland. One of his best friends was a regular at the club playing exhibitions – Alex Higgins. Alex helped Tommy make the club a huge success and other players followed suit becoming regulars at the two clubs Tom owned by the late 1980s. In the 1990s Tommy fell foul of the tax man and the recession, and reluctantly had to close the clubs.

Tommy still plays snooker these days, and is still respected as a good opponent by most professionals. He designed his own special 'little helper' in the form of a special rest for his cue. The rest is a clip-in piece that he slides into his false arm. There are no rules in snooker to determine if this is okay or, in fact, if the length of the rest has any limitations. Tommy has an interesting anecdote that he tells people about a night he had out with Higgins in the Tower Hotel in Dublin in 1982. Apparently an argument broke out on the dance floor between Alex and a couple of men. Fists went flying and Tommy ran from the bar to assist Alex, as he hit one of the men who was battering Alex, his arm went flying and one of the women nearby thought it had been sliced off, and fainted.

SOME YOU WIN . . . SOME YOU LOSE

Ronnie O'Sullivan won his first 28 matches after turning professional. Stephen Hendry lost his first 4 matches as a pro. Both turned pro when they were sixteen years old.

DEAD PARROTT?

The biggest winning margin of victory in a World Championship Final happened in 1989. The match was between John Parrott and Steve Davis, unfortunately Steve wiped the floor with John to an embarrassing 18–3 victory, ouch!

YEAH? WELL BALLS TO YOU AN' ALL, MATE!

An American inventor came up with the ideal solution to the construction of the billiard ball in about 1868. New York chemist John Wesley Hyatt mixed cellulose nitrate camphor and ground-up animal bones to make a formula that he then patented as Celluloid. It was eventually picked up by the film industry, dentists and piano makers to make products that were used every day in the home and industry. The consistency of the material ensured that all the balls in a set were of the same density and size. Hyatt set up The Albany Ball Company to produce the balls en masse, although they often used to explode when hit fiercely as there was not much elasticity in them to spread the impact of the force when the balls met. Ivory balls were still quite popular in the better clubs as players preferred them – perhaps because they didn't explode causing damage to the tables and making a mess.

SHORT AND SWEET:
THE MALTA CUP

The Malta Cup ran for just 4 years from 2005 to 2008.

2005	Stephen Hendry	9–7	Graeme Dott
2006	Ken Doherty	9–8	John Higgins
2007	Shaun Murphy	9–4	Ryan Day
2008	Shaun Murphy	9–3	Ken Doherty

HIGGINS BY NAME, BUT NOT BY NATURE

Some infamous quotes by John Higgins:

I didn't make a 147 until a few years ago. I just wasn't the sort of player who went for them. But it's like buses I suppose, one comes along and then a few more follow.

It's been frustrating these past few years; but I feel that now I'm cueing as well as ever.

'RIGHT' SAID FRED . . .
'I'M NOT TOO SEXY TO WIN!'

Fred Davis played in his first World Championship in 1937 and everyone who attended was excited at the prospect of seeing him play some superb snooker. However it wasn't to be Fred's best display of his skills as he lost 17–14 to Welshman J.A. Withers, a virtually unknown player, in the first round. His brother, however, was Joe Davis who took this as being a bit of a slur on the family name. Joe got revenge for Fred and recovered the family honour, and in style, when he almost whitewashed the helpless Withers 30–1 in the second round. After the event ended, Fred decided to get an eye check up as he was having difficulty focusing. It turned out the he was suffering from myopia, so an optician fitted him out with glasses, and shortly afterwards he re-established himself as one of the best all-round players of his generation.

DID YOU KNOW THAT . . . ?

Ronnie O'Sullivan's middle name is Antonio.

RONNIE O'SULLIVAN: A BRIEF BIOGRAPHY

Ronnie was born on 5 December 1975 in Wordsley, West Midlands. He grew up in the wealthy Essex town of Chigwell and attended Wanstead High School where he was reported to have been a good student. At the age of six he was watching the snooker semi-final between Jimmy White and Alex Higgins with his dad who is a huge snooker fan. Ronnie became hooked and couldn't wait to watch the final between Alex Higgins and Ray Reardon. After the gripping win by Higgins, young Ronnie vowed to become a champion snooker player and to meet his new heroes Higgins, White and Reardon.

By the age of ten Ronnie was already making 100 breaks, encouraged by his dad and uncles who were all excellent boxers. Although he was playing snooker every spare moment he had, he always made the effort to keep up his school work. By the age of fifteen he was a player to be reckoned with and was regarded by many people as the next snooker wonder. At the tender age of just sixteen he turned professional, but didn't win a title until the next year, 1993. That year he won the UK Championship beating Stephen Hendry in the finals. Stephen Hendry was the youngest ever professional – beating Ronnie by just a few months to that record. However, when Ronnie beat Hendry in the 1993 UK Championship he became the youngest ever player to win a ranking title.

The 'Essex Exocet', the 'Rocket' and the 'Magician' are all nicknames attached to Ronnie. He plays like a man possessed sometimes and has an incredible ability to pocket balls at lightning speed. He holds many records, and, with winnings estimated in 2008 at some £6m in tournaments, Ronnie is one of the most prominent sportsmen of his game and era. Add to that his prize money for knocking in 147s at major tournaments and his personal appearance fees, the amount of his earnings climbs into tens of millions. He has, to date in his short career, won 21 ranking titles and 22 ranking events.

In 2001 he won his first World Championship, beating John Higgins in the final 18–14. He also won his third UK Championship title against Ken Doherty 10–1 that same year. Ronnie started the 2002 season with a well-deserved No. 1 ranking.

Like his hero Alex Higgins, Ronnie hasn't been without controversial publicity. At the 1996 World Championships he assaulted media official Mike Ganley – the WPBSA governing body fined him £20,000 and gave him a suspended sentence of a two-year ban. In a gesture of good faith to show he was truly sorry, he also donated £10,000 to charity. In 1998 he won the Benson & Hedges Irish Masters, winning £90,000 and the title. He was later found to have failed a drug test when cannabis traces were found in a random sample. He was stripped of his title and prize money. However, his opponent in the final, Ken Doherty, insisted that Ronnie won the round fair and square. Ken handed back the trophy in protest, but kept the prize money which he considered to be a fair gesture.

During his match against Mark Selby in the Maplin UK Championship in 2007, Ronnie made another 147 and won enough money to be able to buy his dream car outright, a Bentley Continental. He wanted one from the first time he spotted his mate Jimmy White driving one.

RULES IS RULES . . . NOW PAY UP MATEY!

Towards the end of the nineteenth century, a need for some consistency in the rules of the game was necessary. There was no single authority that represented the sport, and with gambling becoming attached to the game, there was a need to have some set rules that would be adhered to for every billiard hall in the country. Without a governing body controlling the development of the game, a wide variety of minor rule variations came to be applied in almost every public billiard room. The initial pressure came from amateur players, with heavy wagers becoming more common, individual arguments were being referred to the sporting press to govern over. The *Sportsman* newspaper was regarded as one of the most reliable authorities for settling such disputes. It wasn't uncommon for a committee of sports writers and editors to be convened to pass judgement on a dispute involving a heavy wager. Among the hundreds of letters received by the newspaper was this one, written to the editor in 1872. It involved a game of Pool and the editor it seems didn't take it all that seriously. It read:

Sir. During a game an excitable friend of mine played out of turn, with the wrong ball, at the wrong ball, used the rest instead of his cue and at the same time made a foul by touching another ball with his arm. What ought to be done under these circumstances?

The editor wrote a reply which was published the next day:

Sir. Have his head shaved and a strong poultice applied to the back of his head.

WE DO RON, RON, RON . . . WE DO RON, RON

Quotes from the 'Wise Old Owl of Snooker', Chairman Ron(nie O'Sullivan):

I noticed more and more people gathering around me. I had absolutely no idea I had converted to Islam and handed my life over to it.

I know what I want to do and there's no point giving my secrets away.

I haven't practiced all season really, I've just been going through the motions.

At the moment I'm not really interested, but don't get me wrong, I want to win!

It wouldn't have been such a terrible thing if I had lost on a first-round match.

My heart's not been in it this year, and I've not been playing well, though I do keep on winning.

A HURRICANE BLOWS DRACULA AWAY!

One of the most popular matches ever played was the final frame of the 1982 World Championship at The Crucible in Sheffield on 16 May. The match was between Alex Higgins and Ray Reardon, the starting score was 17–5 to Higgins, and he had managed to win the last 3 frames with Reardon scoring just 9 points from the 3 frames. All Alex had to do was to win this frame for the title, but the law of averages was against him, although not the laws of Alex Higgins who has an uncanny ability to defy most things.

The frame started with Alex potting a red. He wanted to leave the black in a position for easy potting, but the cue ball ended up on the other side of two reds. Alex had to go between the reds to pot the black and at the same time set up the next red. It worked and he was on his way to a magnificent victory with a breathtaking break of 139 to Reardon's score of 0. Reardon however did make a record as the oldest player to reach a final at the age of 49 years and 7 months old.

A NICKNAME BY ANY OTHER: 20 MORE OF THE FINEST MONIKERS

Ali Carter	The Captain
Alan McManus	Angles
Anthony Hamilton	The Sheriff of Pottingham, Swampy, The Robin Hood of Snooker,
Jamie Cope	The Shotgun
Joe Perry	The Fen Potter, The Gentleman, Joe 'start up slow' Perry
Mark King	The Royal King, The Romford Battler
Neil Robertson	The Melbourne Machine, Thunder from Down Under
Stephen Lee	The Man with the Rolls-Royce Cue Action
Shaun Murphy	The Whiston Warrior, The Magician
John Rea	King of the Baize
Liang Wenbo	The Fearless, Will He Stay or Will He Go, The Rice Man, Lemming

John Higgins	The Wizard of Wishaw,
	The Maximum Man, Haggis
James Troughton	The Leighton Bromswold Bomber
Ian McCullock	The Preston Potter,
	The Pride of Preston
Fergal O'Brien	The Silent Assassin,
	The Baby-Faced Assassin
Eddie Charlton	Steady Eddie
David Gray	The Atom, Casper
Dominic Dale	The Spaceman
Cliff Thorburn	The Grinder
Bill Werbeniuk	Big Bill

THE FIRST EVER TOTAL CLEARANCE

Sidney Smith is considered to be the first snooker player ever to perform a total clearance. It was during an exhibition event in Derbyshire on 10 December 1936. The clearance of 133 was a world record, but Smith lost most of the publicity opportunities to the other great story of the time, the abdication of King Edward VIII. He once said that he could never forgive Mrs Simpson, it was generally taken that he was referring to the loss of publicity and not the loss of the king. Smith was also a pioneer of training films for snooker players – his films can still be seen today on YouTube.

A RECORD, BUT NOT FOR LONG . . .

Sidney Smith didn't hold the record break title for long, as just a week later in Sydney, Australia, Horace Lindrum performed a 141 break. He held the record until 1946 when Walter Donaldson beat it by just 1 point.

RIGHT ON CUE

Joe Davis was the first world champion to have a cue named after him; it is now know as the Peradon Joe Davis Cue and is made by Peradon Ltd.

JOE DAVIS: A BRIEF BIOGRAPHY

Joe was born in Whitwell, Derbyshire, on 15 April 1901 into a coal-mining family. His father Fred and his mother Elizabeth Ann didn't want their first born to be restricted to a life down the pits, so in 1903 they took the license of the Travellers Rest pub in Whittington Moor. In 1910 they moved to the Queens Hotel and it was here that Joe Davis' billiards and snooker ambitions were born.

The hotel had a snooker table and Joe used to watch the best of the area's players strutting their stuff. Just four years later, at the age of fourteen, he got a job working in a local snooker hall, which was a year after he had won the local Derbyshire Billiards Championship. It was common in those pre-First World War days for people to start work at fourteen. Little did the hustlers know that this fresh-faced youngster was already a natural on the snooker table.

Joe Davis was so good at snooker and billiards that just one year after European hostilities ended, he turned professional. In 1926 he won his way to the final of the World Billiards Championship, his opponent being the reigning champion Tom Newman. Joe lost that first attempt at the championship, but told his dad that he would get it the next year. In 1927 he again reached the final, again against Tom Newman, and was again defeated. He again swore that he would come back the following year and win the title. He made good another promise though that same year – he won the World Snooker Title in 1927. He actually helped to organise the event, and then went on to beat Tom Dennis 20–10 in a nail-biting final. His prize money was just £6 10s, but Joe didn't care about that.

In 1928 he again played his way to the final of the World Billiards Championship to face, you guessed it, Tom Newman. This time Joe won and he was now the World Champion in both billiards and snooker.

Joe Davis went on to become the most successful snooker and billiards champion to date – no-one has come anywhere near to his incredible record. His brother Fred Davis was also an accomplished player and champion in both sports.

Joe was married twice, first in 1921 to Florence Stevenson at Chesterfield Methodist Church. The cost of his fame as a British sportsman, and a favourite on the tournament and exhibition circuit, took its toll on his marriage and he had many affairs. In 1940 Florence finally had enough and divorced him. He moved to London and married June Milo in 1945. Joe started to take it easy then and ended up doing a lot of charity work, exhibitions and focusing on supporting Derby County Football Club.

Joe was awarded the OBE for his contribution to sport and his charity work in 1963. His car was easily recognisable as it had the registration number CUE 1. He was a famous figure in the Sports Hall of Fame at Madame Tussauds. In 1955 he made a record 147 snooker break at an exhibition match at the Leicester Square Hall, London, a first in snooker history for an exhibition frame.

Joe Davis is considered the father of modern snooker. He died peacefully at his home in Hampshire on 10 July 1978. His widow June died on her ninety-eighth birthday on 23 July 2008.

WHAT THEY SAY ABOUT EACH OTHER!

Neil Robertson on beating Stephen Hendry:
Any time when you play Stephen Hendry it's going to be a big game. People point out that he's not playing at his best any more but he's still a really top-class player. It was a high-quality match. I'm relieved to win and really looking forward to playing Stephen Maguire in the next round. I wasn't around that much when Stephen Hendry was winning everything, but I was surprised with the amount of easy balls he missed in our match.

Ali Carter after a 6–0 demolition of Peter Ebdon:
I'm focussing on keeping things simple, and I'm enjoying the game. It was a good performance tonight against a top player who always makes it tough for you. My long game is good at the moment. If there's a ball available I'll try to pot it, and I seem to get more than I miss. It's a strong asset to have.

Mark Allen had some interesting things to say about Ronnie O'Sullivan:
Maybe it's what the game needs, let him quit. Ronnie sometimes says things without properly thinking about them, and then it has repercussions. He wouldn't be where he is today without snooker – he was wrong for what he said. There are plenty of top snooker players today. Snooker doesn't just need Ronnie. What else would he do if he quit? You can't see him doing a nine-to-five job. He'd rather be playing snooker. I don't play snooker to win money. I want to win tournaments. Everyone has to pay the bills but if you win titles then the money takes care of itself.

Mark Selby after his narrow win over Ricky Walden:
I knew it would be tough and perhaps I put too much pressure on myself to win, rather than just trying to enjoy it. I've lost a few deciding frames this season so it was good to prove to myself that when the pressure is on I can still make important breaks.

John Higgins on a win over Marco Fu:
If I'd had a spare cue then I would have probably smashed mine too. That's how bad I was feeling because I really

should have been in front. Marco turned the screw and should have gone 5–2, and then I would have been in trouble. Thankfully he gave me a chance and I managed to get back into the match.

Ding Junhui said this about Shaun Murphy:
It's a good result to beat Shaun for the first time, especially as he's just become UK champion. I just tried to enjoy the game because I don't like the pressure.

Stephen Maguire on a win over Graeme Dott:
I feel I can finally relax now. I think I don't play again until Thursday. I'm in two minds about whether to head up the road or stay down. I'm just relieved really. He never missed a long ball until he was 5–2 up. Then he missed a couple. He has not won a lot of matches, but you can tell he's starting to get more confidence about him. The way he's zipping around the table, it's like the old Graeme.

And Stephen Maguire on those match-fixing allegations:
I read the papers as much as everybody else. Luckily enough I'm very, very thick-skinned. If I get a phone call, I get a phone call. I'll help them out whatever they want to do. I know there's nothing to worry about so it's not really bothered me too much. It's not nice. Jamie's a good friend of mine. But I'm 100 per cent sure there's nothing wrong, so we'll just wait and see. If I had something to hide then maybe it would bother me but I've got absolutely nothing to hide.

DID YOU KNOW THAT . . . ?

The reason traditional tables have a green coloured cloth is to commemorate the origins of the game. Originally it was played on manicured lawns as a stick and ball game.

THE GERMAN MASTERS

The German Masters tournament ran from 1995 until 1998. Not one German player got into the final. It was dominated by British players and one Canadian. It was a ranking event known as the German Open from 1995–7 before it became the German Masters in 1998.

1995	John Higgins	9–3	Ken Doherty
1996	Ronnie O'Sullivan	9–7	Alain Robidoux
1997	John Higgins	9–4	John Parrott
1998	John Parrott	6–4	Mark J. Williams

HE SAID WHAT? THE CHEEKY GET!

Someone once threw a petrol bomb at Alex Higgins . . . and he drank it!

Comedian Frank Carson

BISH BOSH, WHITEWASH

One of the most talked about whitewash games happened at The Crucible (of all places!) during round one of the 1992 World Championship competition. Eddie Charlton was drawn against John Parrott and came to the table full of confidence. Parrott wiped the floor with his opponent when he performed like a 'man who had sold his soul to the Devil.' He whitewashed a demoralised Charlton 10–0. Ouch!

MORE OF THOSE SILLY BLOOPERS!

When you start off, it's usually nil-nil.

Steve Davis

Just enough points here for Tony to pull the cat out of the fire.

Ray Edmonds

Tony Meo is beginning to find his potting boots.

Rex Williams

Suddenly Alex Higgins is 7–0 down.

David Vine

From this position you've got to fancy either yourself, or your opponent winning.

Kirk Stevens

The match has gradually and suddenly, come to a climax.

David Vine

No one came closer to winning the title last year than the runner-up.

Dennis Taylor

I've always said the difference between winning and losing is nothing at all.

Terry Griffiths

Well, valour was the better part of discretion there.

Jack Karnehm

Sometimes the deciding frame is always the hardest one to win.

Dennis Taylor

That said, the inevitable failed to happen.

John Pulman

10–4, and that could mean exactly what it means.

David Vine

And now for some snooker news: Steve Davis has crashed out of the UK Billiards Championship.

Allan Taylor

Ray Reardon is one of the great Crucible champions. He won it five times when the championship was played away from The Crucible.

David Vine

RECORD-BREAKER DALE

Dominic Dale holds the record for the highest number of points scored during a single frame. It happened in round one of the 1999 Embassy World Championship. The frame was against Nigel Bond and the fans were amazed to be witnesses to this moment in snooker history. Dominic's score was made up as such: potted balls 123 off a break of 122 and 1 red, then Nigel made 11 consecutive misses worth another 44 points making a record-making total for Dominic of 167.

A TAXING TIME FOR THE GAME

'Big' Bill Werbeniuk was notorious in the snooker world for his ability to sink vast amounts of beer before, during and after a frame. He successfully fought the tax man for the right to claim his beer bills against taxable earnings. His argument was that he needed Beta-Blockers to steady his nerves and, after the WPBSA banned them, he claimed he needed the beer to make him play with consistency.

BORN IN A BAIZE OF GLORY

Both snooker and billiard tables are covered with a cloth which is often referred to as felt because of its similar texture to that particular material. Modern day cloths are actually a woven worsted or wool and nylon blend called baize. Cloth has been used to cover billiards tables since the fifteenth century. In fact the forerunner of the most famous maker of billiard cloth, Iwan Simonis, is thought to have been established in 1453.

Bar or pub tables which get a lot of play, use a slower, more durable cloth. The cloth used in pool and snooker halls, and on home billiard-room tables is faster. This cloth provides less friction, allowing the balls to roll further across the table bed. Competition-quality pool cloth is also made from 100 per cent worsted wool. Snooker cloth traditionally has a nap, that is to say consistent fibre directionality. This causes the balls to behave differently when rolling against the nap.

The cloth of the billiard table has traditionally been green, reflecting its origins as a lawn game, and has been so coloured since the sixteenth century. However, it is now also produced in other colours such as red and blue to reflect the most common colours used in international flags.

QUEUEING FOR A PERFECT CUE

Billiards and snooker games are mostly played with a stick known as a cue. A cue is usually either a one-piece tapered stick, or a two-piece stick divided in the middle by a joint. This allows the cue to be stored and carried more easily in a case. High quality cues are generally two pieces and are made of a hardwood, generally maple for billiards and ash for snooker.

The butt end of the cue is of a larger circumference and is intended to be gripped by a player's hand. The shaft of the cue is of a smaller circumference, usually tapering to 0.4 or 0.55 inch (11–14mm) to an end called a ferrule. The ferrule is usually made of fibreglass or brass. In the top of this is screwed a rounded leather tip on a brass base. This is designed to be flush with the ferrule, to make the final contact with the ball. The tip, in conjunction with chalk, can be used to impart spin to the cue ball when it is not hit in its centre.

Cheaper cues are generally made of pine or low-grade maple. It is also sometimes made from Ramin – an endangered species of rainforest hardwood. A quality cue can be expensive and may be made of exotic woods and other expensive materials which are artfully inlaid into decorative patterns. Many modern cues are also made like golf clubs, with high-tech materials such as woven graphite.

Skilled players may use more than one cue during a game, including a separate, generally lighter cue for the opening break shot. This is because of the cue speed gained from a lighter stick. Another, shorter cue, with a special tip for jump shots is also used by some players.

YOU CAN CHALK THAT ONE UP TO . . .

A layer of chalk is applied to the tip of the cue stick, often before every shot, to increase the tip's friction efficiency. When it impacts against the cue ball on a non-centred hit, it prevents a miscue (an unintentional slippage between the cue tip and the cue ball) happening. Cue tip chalk is made from a combination of substances. These can be calcium carbonate, also known as calcite, or carbonate of lime, and any other of several proprietary compounds, with a silicate base. Cue chalk may also refer to a cone of fine, white hand chalk similar to talcum powder. This is generally used to reduce friction between the cue and bridge hand during a shot. Some brands of hand chalk are actually made of compressed talc. Cue tip chalk cannot be used for this purpose because it is too abrasive, and is hand-staining and difficult to apply. Many players prefer a slick pool glove over the use of hand chalk or talc.

Cue tip chalk was first used by straight rail billiard pro William A. Spinks, and was developed with his chemist friend William Hoskins in 1897. It is made by crushing silica and the abrasive substance corundum or aloxite, also known as aluminium oxide, into a powder. It is then dyed green or blue-green like traditional billiard cloth.

Modern-day cue chalk is available in a multitude of colours and is bound with glue. Each manufacturer's brand has different qualities which can significantly affect play. High humidity can also impair the effectiveness of cue chalk. Harder, drier compounds are generally considered superior by most professional players.

HE SAID WHAT?

Billiards is very similar to snooker, except there are only three balls and no one ever watches it.

Steve Davis

THE BILLIARD TABLE

In among the papers and will of the French King Louis XI, dated around 1450, is a document that tells us that a billiard table similar to the modern ones existed. Before the seventeenth century, little is actually known about the sport. However from drawings before 1600 we do know that at times the lawn game was brought indoors. They set up a large board on a dining table and simply turfed it. The Europeans, especially the French and the Italians, added cushions of stuffed straw when the billiards table finally came into being. It was in the mid-nineteenth century that furniture-makers were approached to custom-make tables, and some of these original tables still exist today, although you would be forbidden from playing on them. These tables were the first ones to have a slate bed, which replaced the solid wooden bed bases.

One of the first English table makers was John Thurston. He experimented with slate beds as early as 1826. Thurston was also responsible for introducing rubber cushions in 1835. At that time furniture makers who had turned table makers were still using the same traditional materials they used in chairs and settees. These materials included horse hair, feathers and even old recycled rags. Even so, Thurston's rubber cushions weren't that good. As mentioned earlier, the temperature in the room made them hard or soft and that made the game inconsistent. Cushion warmers were patented by Thurston, but even these weren't that successful and many table makers still used the old traditional material. However, when Thomas Hancock patented his method for 'Vulcanising' rubber in 1835, Thurston's were the first to use that type of rubber on tables. His first set of vulcanised rubber cushions were presented to Queen Victoria and Prince Albert, and fitted to their table at Windsor Castle.

In America the mass production of billiard tables didn't really get going until about 1845. In that year a company called Brunswick-Balke-Collender started mass production. By 1892 companies on the west coast had started up in San Francisco as the game became more popular there.

ACCORDING TO MURPHY'S LAW: QUOTES FROM SHAUN MURPHY

I was feeling terrible and I was all over the place, and they do say in these matches that the intervals come at the right time or the wrong time. I was like a heavyweight swaying on my feet. That interval came at just the right time, and my manager also said some really good things to me.

Win, lose or draw, I'm having a lot of fun.

In the words of Terry Griffiths, 'I'm in the final now.'

There are not many players who can say they've had the privilege of playing in the Masters. This is the first year I've got there on merit, and I'm really looking forward to it.

Wembley is a class arena and walking out there with just one table and, hopefully, a good audience is something to really cherish.

I decided I was going to try to win, and that's exactly what I did.

Crafty Ken beat me 10–9 in the World Championship a couple of years ago, so it'll be nice to get one over on him.

The fact was it was 14–14 in the semi-final of the World Championship. Yes, I'd lost seven on the bounce but it was the best of five for a place in the final and that thought completely changed my perspective.

I first started playing when I was eight. I got a little snooker table for Christmas. It was only 4ft-something from Toys 'R' Us.

OK, the number of tournaments has been cut down due to a lack of funds, but all the ones we have now pay for themselves, and don't owe anyone any money.

THE PRIZE FOR BEST (USELESS) IDEA GOES TO: STEVE DAVIS OBE

Fewer frames go to the colours because everyone's so bloody good. My solution: The inclusion of a mushroom on the table. If you knock it over your score would go back to zero points.

PAUL ALAN HUNTER: A BRIEF BIOGRAPHY

In loving memory of a great husband, father and player.

When Paul Hunter tragically lost his fight against cancer, his family lost a loving dad, husband and son; the city of Leeds lost a great ambassador; snooker lost a legend and the fans lost their hero. Paul took up snooker late in life when you compare him to other greats such as Jimmy White, Alex Higgins, Ray Reardon and Joe Johnson, who also coached him. He knew his weak points and worked tirelessly on overcoming them to become the champion that he was. He once said that he learned from all his snooker heroes by watching them over and over again on the TV. Born on 14 October 1978, Paul turned professional at just sixteen years old in 1995. He soon became a favourite with the players and the fans, and was nicknamed the 'Beckham of the Baize' due to his good looks and professionalism.

He wasn't an instant winner and didn't win his first ranking title until 1998 – the Regal Welsh Open – which he won by beating the World Champion John Higgins 9–5 in the final. His prize money was £60,000. He also won the title of Young Player of the Year which is awarded each year by the Snooker Writers' Association. In 1999 he played at The Crucible for the first of many times although he was knocked out early in the competition, putting it down to bad luck. He vowed to improve his game, and went away from Sheffield having made himself a promise to win the championship one day.

Titles seemed to elude Paul as he bettered his game. He ended up higher in the tournaments but never seemed to get beyond the quarter-finals in most of them. He used to say to journalists that he still had a bit to learn, but time to learn it.

By 2001 Paul was going for gold. His play had improved so much that he quickly went through Matthew Stevens, Peter Ebdon and Stephen Hendry to win a place against

Fergal O'Brien in the Masters final. Fergal wasn't about to grant Paul any quarter, and he made the Yorkshire lad work for his prize money. Paul triumphed by winning the nineteenth frame 10–9 which clinched him the winner's cheque of £175,000. He also gave the fans a superb evening's entertainment by knocking in four centuries during the final. In the after-match press interviews, Paul made his girlfriend Lindsey Fell turn bright red as he revealed that during the final break in play he and Lindsey had 'a bonk' in the hotel bedroom. He went on to say that it must have taken all his tension away, because when he returned to the table he managed those four centuries in just six frames.

The following year was to be his best to date as he returned to the Masters and again went through the rounds like a dose of salts, ending up in the final against Mark Williams. The match wasn't going Paul's way though, and he quickly went down 5–0. Maybe the 'Plan B' he used the previous year came into play again during a break, because he quickly recovered and eventually beat Mark 10–9. The score was the same one with which he won the title in the previous season, but the cheque he went away with was bigger – a whopping £190,000. In winning the title for the second time in a row, he also attained legendary status by joining Stephen Hendry and Cliff Thorburn as the third player to win the title consecutively.

Paul also won the Regal Welsh Open again that year, beating Ken Doherty in the final. Ken had beaten Paul in the final in 2001, so he felt that he had got his revenge over the Irishman.

2003 saw Paul back at the Embassy World Championship and all fired up to win the title. He certainly deserved to win it as he devoured all his challengers to reach the semi-finals to face Ken Doherty. Paul left the evening's play 15–9 up on the 'Dublin Darlin', and returned the next day to greet a down-in the-mouth Ken. However, the 'Dublin Rascal' wasn't giving in so easily and astounded the fans – and Paul – with a straight eight-frame win. Paul was again denied his final, but vowed again to return the next year and take the trophy home with him.

He married Lindsey in 2004 in Jamaica, and their daughter Evie Rose made him a proud dad on Boxing Day, 2005. The joy of fatherhood was tinged with a great sadness, though, as Paul had announced to the world just eight months earlier that he was suffering from a rare cancer causing neuroendocrine tumours. He needed chemotherapy and the treatment kept him out of snooker until his untimely death just over a year later. The day that devastated his family and fans the world over was 9 October 2006 as, on that day, Paul fell asleep and never woke up. His funeral in the city centre of Leeds was like a royal affair, snooker's most famous faces coming from far and wide to say a sad farewell to a brave father, husband and son as well as a friend to them all. World Snooker chairman Sir Rodney Walker spoke from the pulpit to a packed church, and an even bigger crowd outside. 'I'm sure that everyone who met Paul, as well as his millions of fans and the sporting public as a whole, will join me in sending most sincere sympathies to Lindsey, Paul's parents, his family and friends. Paul was a man who had everything going for him; an outstanding talent, good looks, fame, riches, charm and a beautiful wife. This shows us just how quickly life can change. It's a bitter blow for snooker but most importantly for his family and our thoughts are with them.'

Lindsey has written a book about her life with Paul and prior to the Premier League Snooker matches on 12 October 2006, players Jimmy White, Ronnie O'Sullivan, Ken Doherty and Ding Junhui, along with referee Alan Chamberlain and commentators Willie Thorne and Phil Yates, all stood for a moment of silence to remember him. There was also a short video tribute.

Fellow professionals Stephen Hendry, Mark Williams, Jimmy White, Matthew Stevens and Ken Doherty have led calls for the Masters trophy to be named in Hunter's memory. The WPBSA announced shortly afterwards that the players' wishes would be granted and Paul Hunter is now remembered forever. As a final gesture to the impact of his untimely death on snooker, Lindsey set up the Paul Hunter Foundation to assist disabled and able-bodied youngsters to be able to play the sport.

POKER FACE, YOU'VE GOT THE CUTEST LITTLE POKER FACE

Many snooker players have turned to playing poker in tournaments around the world. Many of them are now poker superstars as well as snooker playing stars. Matthew Stevens started playing the game in 1992 after seeing Jimmy White and Steve Davis playing. In December 2004 Matthew won a tournament in the 888.com Pacific Poker

Open. His prize, after beating darts champion Phil Taylor and tennis star Yevgeny Kafelnikov, was a staggering £260,000, or in US dollars – $500,000.

BILLIARDS AMERICANO

The American billiards industry owes its popularity and wealth, to an incredible Irishman named Michael Phelan. Known across the pond as the 'Father of American Billiards', Phelan emigrated from Ireland and wrote the first American book on the game. He was typically a writer anyway and went to America to make his fortune as a fiction author. During his early years in New York he began to hang around the billiards halls and soon became fascinated by the game. He became a huge influence on the game when he started writing about it for local newspapers. His billiards expertise gave him the advantage of being able to devise rules, and set-out standards of table etiquette. Phelan was also an amateur inventor, and is responsible for adding diamonds to the table to help players aim more effectively. His inventing head helped to developed new table and cushion designs that revolutionised the sport. He was the first American billiards columnist and his expertise really arose from the voice he had in print. On New Year's Day, 1859, his first article was published by *Frank Leslie's Illustrated Weekly*. In March, Phelan won the pot prize of $15,000 when he won a championship competition in Detroit. This was the first ever stake match organised in America. In his role as a promoter of the game, he was respected by the furniture companies who made the tables. After being approached by a maker of billiard tables to become a board member, he decided to start his own company and Phelan & Collender was born. Hugh W. Collender was Phelan's son-in-law as well as his partner.

Their factory on Tenth Avenue in Manhattan extended the full length between 36th and 37th streets. They made billiard balls and markers and between 700 and 1,000 billiard tables each year. By 1872, the factory was three times bigger than any other billiard products maker in the world. In 1884 they merged with J.M. Brunswick & Balke and formed the Brunswick-Balke-Collender Company. They were so big in the game of billiards that they controlled most of the influence in the game until the 1950s. That company was in turn succeeded by Brunswick Billiards, which is still the biggest American manufacturer.

FANCY A GAME OF POOL? YOU BET I DO!

Billiards is thought to have been brought to America by the Dutch and Italian settlers in the eighteenth century. They started off playing the European version, and then after the War of Independence it started to deviate off onto a tangent of its own. The most popular version played between 1780 and 1870 was called 'Four Ball Billiards', it was played on a 12ft long table with only 4 pockets cut into each corner. As the name indicates it had two white and two red balls in total, there were various ways to notch up points and it was possible to get up to 13 points for just one shot.

It was a strange game by the modern standards that we play to. It was a mix of cannons where the balls were also potted. By 1876 the Americans were celebrating their first century of independence, and the billiards halls had two types of tables in them, the most popular was a pocket-less table on which the forerunner of Carom was played, with three balls. 'Fifteen Ball Pool' was the other game and it eventually overtook Carom as the most popular. The halls soon came to the notice of the criminal element, and illegal gambling crept into the game. Punters made bets ante-post on the eventual winner, and also side bets throughout a game on individual pots. As a 'Pool of Bets' was involved in the game, the name changed to pool. Today in America you will find pool halls where the game of pool is played, but in the corrupt times of New York and other major cities, a pool hall was originally a betting office. As the information on results was sometimes delayed, the gangsters running the offices installed pool tables so the punters could while away the time. From this simple idea came more betting opportunities, and so the gangsters invested in pool halls to legitimise their ill-gotten gains.

IS THAT JUST A LOAD OF BALLS OR WHAT?

In Fifteen Ball Pool the maximum points is 120, and unlike today you didn't have a 'spot' or a 'colour' to pot, both players just went for any ball. The balls were numbered 1 to 15 and you got the number of points for a ball you potted. Obviously you don't have to be Einstein to work out that when a player scored 61 points, he was declared the winner as it wasn't possible to make a 'snooker'. This game is widely believed to have been devised for gambling purposes, as players got through games quite quickly. It was therefore inevitable that it would become the most popular version and this was encouraged when the first tournaments were played in American halls. By the 1870s competitions were rife in every state and the game got the nickname '61 Pool' for obvious reasons. In October 1878 a Canadian named Cyrille Dion became the first American Pool Champion. He sadly died a few months later of lung cancer, and this was put down to the smoke he breathed in during long days in halls.

By 1888 the game was losing popularity, so the rules were changed to make it more interesting. Instead of winning the frame by scoring points, the rules now said that the player who potted the most balls was the winner. This revived the interest and the version was adopted by all the halls. 'Continuous Pool' then came in when the rules changed again a few years later. This allowed a player to carry his points from one frame to the next one. In order to be able to do so, all he had to do was to knock in the last ball. Competition rules also changed to reflect the many versions being brought in and by the 1920s eight, nine and straight pool were also being played across America. Different states adopted different versions, which made the inter-state competitions that more interesting.

NICE ONE CYRILLE, NICE ONE SON

Cyrille Dion was born in Montreal in March 1843. He completed his education and became a bookkeeper and stock controller for a grocery store in the city. His leisure time was spent playing billiards, and he became a well-known amateur champion. In 1863 he won the equivalent of the Canadian Amateur Billiards Championship and turned professional in July 1865. It was after he won the Championship of Canada, played in Montreal over a seven-day event, that he ventured into being a touring champion of the sport, going on to beat the local and state champions of fifteen states in America.

In 1870 he moved to New York to make his name in the sporting circles of the city. His first big win in New York was beating the American champion John McDevitt by one point to become the new Champion of America. He then went to San Francisco and was beaten by just 14 points in a tournament by John Deery. Then he won the 4-ball Championship, becoming the proud holder of the 'Diamond Cue' – the 4-ball equivalent of the championship trophy. However, he was the 4-ball American champion for just eighteen months. His game was inconsistent and he went from favourite to being forgotten in his short career. He died at his mother's house after catching a chill on a draughty train – ironically he was travelling home to allow his mother to nurse him back to health, after catching another severe chill in New York.

DON'T 'HUSTLE' ME FOR THE 'COLOR OF MONEY'

Billiards was revived by two Hollywood-related events, one in 1961 and the other in 1986. The first was in the form of the Paul Newman movie *The Hustler*, which is based on the novel by Walter Tevis. The film noir depiction of the dark life of a pool hustler's life was portrayed by Paul Newman as the eponymous hero of the movie. The quietness of the tense scenes was suddenly interrupted by the sound of clicking balls in an almost Hitchcock-style manner, and it sent America into a new billiard frenzy. Pool halls started opening up again all over the country. This continued through the decade and was only interrupted by the Vietnam War. Outside events like Woodstock and the American fad of keeping fit by jogging around the streets and parks, finally led to another decline in the sport. By 1985 there were only two public pool rooms left in Manhattan – this was down from 2,765 during the years before the Second World War.

In 1986 Hollywood decided to revive the movie with a sequel, and *The Color of Money* was the result. With Paul Newman playing the same role, albeit a lot older, Tom Cruise was brought in to play the 'apprentice' hustler. As the new kid on the block in Hollywood, Cruise brought the excitement of pool and the hustle to a whole new generation. The movie was a huge hit due to the acting, script and tense scenes, along of course with the two Hollywood stars representing two generations. Upper class pool and billiard rooms catering to the *nouvelle riche* of the City of London and Wall Street – who wouldn't have been seen dead in the old-style rooms – sprang up like a Phoenix from the flames. The trend has been more steady in America than Europe, where the sport has been in decline since the mid-1990s. Maybe with players like Jimmy White getting roles in Brit flicks, pool may be revived in the UK again, you never know! After all, the pop stars are all making comebacks and some are doing it very successfully, too.

THE TALE OF THE 'TICKING LUNCH'

Alex Higgins is as well known for his shenanigans as he is for his snooker. Here are a few anecdotes that I got from Alex and his sisters while I was writing his autobiography for him in 2005.

Alex was practicing in the 1970s for his comeback to win the World Championship again. He used to practice at his local snooker hall in Belfast, a time that was at the height of 'The Troubles'. His sisters Ann and Jean used to look after him as Alex was prone to just playing frame after frame. As the snooker halls have no windows in them, players tend to forget the time and hours turn into a full day very quickly.

Now, the girls would make Alex a lunch and wrap it up in brown paper to keep it fresh – it was usually sandwiches and a bit of fruit. They took it in turns to deliver it to the snooker hall as they went into town to do their shopping. One day Ann was in a bit of a hurry and, as she walked into the snooker hall, she saw that no one was at the counter where they usually left the lunches. Being in a hurry to get back home and not wanting to disturb Alex at play, she left the brown paper lunch parcel on the counter and shouted out the back that she was leaving it for Alex. Sometime later the manager came back to the counter and was greeted by the parcel. Now you have to remember that at this time in Belfast everyone was suspicious of unknown, unaccompanied and unidentifiable packages. The various factions all used parcel bombs as a means of getting their message of fear across, so any such parcel was treated with great suspicion. The manager ran into the hall and told everyone that he thought there was a bomb on the counter and they should all go out the back way while he called the bomb squad. Alex as usual was concentrating on his game and was either not listening, or was totally dismissive of the whole affair. The bomb squad arrived in around ten minutes and the officer in charge took a statement from the police who were already in attendance – he was assured that the building had been cleared.

The UXB man was sent in to check out the 'suspicious parcel' – in those days they didn't have the robot devices they use today. He reported back that the suspect bomb wasn't ticking, so therefore it was most likely a device that would explode when picked up or opened. On instructions from the officer in charge, he started cutting the string that was holding it together. It didn't explode so he reported back that it was most likely a trembler trigger that would make it go off when it was moved. It was decided that he was to going to cut his way in using a scalpel, and he returned to the parcel on the counter. With a headset on and a microphone linking him directly to the control centre outside, he started to cut his way in. He got halfway round when suddenly Alex appeared from nowhere and asked him what he was doing. The man told Alex to go outside as he was defusing a bomb. With that, Alex picked up the parcel and says 'Bomb? That's no f***ing bomb, that's my lunch, and I'm not sharing it with you!' The UXB man dropped to the floor expecting the bomb to go off, and watched in amazement as Alex unwrapped it and took a chicken sandwich from it. His officer was screaming through the earphones asking for a report, but the man was totally speechless. Alex wandered outside with the parcel in one hand and a sandwich in the other. As everyone watched in awe, Alex asked if there was a cup of tea to be had. The story made the papers the next day and Ann and Jean always made sure that in future they put a message on the parcel clearly stating it was Alex's lunch.

IN THE 'DEAD OF NIGHT' ONE NIGHT

Jimmy White was influenced, as were so many of our other snooker champions, by Alex Higgins who he met and played at the age of fourteen. Jimmy also has great anecdotes about himself and other snooker players.

Jimmy was devastated when his brother Martin died of cancer (Jimmy himself has also battled the disease). It was decided by the family that they would give Martin a traditional White family send off, which started the day before the funeral in a London pub. The afternoon began with relatives and friends celebrating the life of Martin on the funeral eve, everyone sitting around chatting about the 'good ol' days' and Martin in general. Jimmy started to get a little emotional and his sister was comforting him. 'Martin should be with us today, he always loved a good party,' he said. His sister Jackie had no idea where this was leading, and just thought that Jimmy was rambling with the drink. Trying to reassure him, she agreed that Martin would be proud of the send off, and that he did love a good party. 'Right,' said Jimmy, 'that's it. I'm going to fetch him sis, you coming?' He marched out of the door and down the road to the funeral parlour, with Jackie following in hot pursuit. It was quite dark but Jimmy managed to find his way to the Chapel of Rest entrance at the side of the building. Jackie watched as Jimmy tried the door; it was locked so Jimmy gave it a sharp kick and to their surprise it opened. In they went and found Martin dressed in his best suit, shirt and tie and a hat. Jimmy edged the body up and cradling him he called a mate who often drove him to matches. The mate arrived and helped Jimmy and Jackie carry him into the car, and drove them all back to the pub. Martin was laid out on a couple of tables and they all carried on drinking, raising their glasses to him every now and then. This went on for about five hours and it was now into the early hours. It was then decided that Martin had to go back to the Chapel of Rest, so Jimmy called his mate again. The driver came into the pub and realised that Martin was in fact dead, and refused to drive them back to the parlour. So Jimmy called a black cab and they told the driver that Martin was just unconscious, which worked as the driver held the door open for them as they put Martin into the back.

When they arrived at the funeral parlour, Jimmy took Martin and placed him back in the coffin. He then noticed that the hat was missing and started looking around for it. Just then the police arrived and asked him what he was doing – a neighbour had reported a suspicious character outside the building that appeared to be supporting another man. Jimmy explained the situation and the two officers were quite sympathetic. They were also huge snooker fans and, because no damage had been done, they agreed to let Jimmy walk away and secured the doors. The next few hours were spent sleeping off the previous day's alcohol – but Jimmy needn't have bothered as when he got the drinks bill, that sobered him up even more so. The whole day and night's drinking bill came to £4,578.59, but as Jimmy said, 'Martin would have laughed at the situation, and it was all worth it in the end.'

SMOKING BAN!
WHAT SMOKING BAN, BABE?

Alex Higgins is the subject of so many great stories, but not all of them are as true as they are made out to be.

A writer named Richard Dormer wrote and acted in a play about the life of the man known as the 'Hurricane', and the play was named simply *Hurricane*. The show was well received at the Edinburgh Fringe Festival where Richard won best actor for his portrayal. It was later shown in Sheffield at The Crucible, Belfast and London to rave reviews. Richard reflects that he first met Higgins in the bar of Amiens Street railway station in Dublin. Richard was chatting to his mate about an idea he had to write a biopic play about Alex Higgins; with that his mate shook his head to one side and Richard looked around to see Alex drinking a pint of Guinness while reading the paper. He later said in an interview, 'I was wearing an orange, pigskin leather retro jacket that he insisted he wanted to swap for his jacket, but I didn't give it to him. It was at that moment, when I sensed the danger in him, that I knew I had to write it.'

The play was showing at the London Arts Theatre in 2004, and Alex just happened to be passing by when he saw the posters outside. He later went along to watch it, and while he was sitting in the theatre waiting for the show to start, he lit up a cigarette. By that time in London a smoking ban was in place in cinemas, theatres and the Underground, so when the smoke was spotted, a panicking attendant rushed down to tell the offender to put it out. Alex being Alex he argued that the play was about him and that he was a guest so he should be allowed to be himself. The attendant was having none of it and eventually Alex moved outside to finish his smoke. A myth about this incident was borne by some supposed theatregoers that Alex was smoking a joint, which just added to the intrigue of the play and to Alex's reputation as the wild man of snooker. However, I can tell you that Alex assured me that it was simply a roll up and not a joint. It doesn't really matter anyway as the incident made the nationals, radio and TV news, and the play was an even bigger sell out. Many people, I suspect, were hoping Alex would make an impromptu appearance and create some more havoc, such is the pull of the man.

HANG ON THERE – IS THAT A WIN OR A TIE?

Dennis Taylor is well known for his big glasses and his inimitable Irish humour, but how many people know of his 'tie' to Isadora Duncan, the dancer who was accidentally strangled in 1922 when her scarf became entangled in the rear wheel of the car she was a passenger in.

Dennis Taylor was commentating for the BBC with snooker pundit Clive Everton. They had always got on well and as a pair they worked well together. That is, until the night Clive nearly strangled Dennis with his own tie. It wasn't deliberate of course, but it was still quite frightening for Dennis, especially after Alex Higgins was alleged to have once told him that he would have him shot. During a break in the play, Clive and Dennis chilled out by stretching their legs in the commentary box which was some distance above the floor level. Clive had a habit of leaning against the window of the box. The problem arose when he forgot that the window had been slid back to let in some air – poor Clive went backwards and grabbed at the air for something to catch hold of to stop him from falling out. In his panic to help Clive,

Dennis stepped forward to grab him, but Clive was one step ahead of him and grabbed onto Dennis instead. Unfortunately he grabbed Dennis' tie which was fully done up, and as he fell back even more he gripped the tie even tighter. In the meantime Dennis had tried to step backwards in order to avoid being pulled out with Clive – as he did so he turned on his footing and the full weight of Clive pulled the tie tighter, almost strangling him. So there was Dennis trying to pull away, and Clive trying to stop himself falling out of the window. It had a happy ending, though, when Clive got his balance and managed to get back inside the room. To this day Dennis rarely wears a tie in the commentary box.

I'LL NEVER FORGET . . . ER! WHAT'S HIS NAME?

Alan Hughes is a well known snooker compère, but even they have their bad days and on one occasion Alan wished that he had stayed in bed.

Alan was the compère at one of the many exhibition matches that Alex Higgins and Jimmy White were playing in. Even compères have their off days, and Alex Higgins isn't one you want to have a bad day with. Alan was always aware that the crowds loved the build up of the players' introductions, and when Alex played Jimmy at exhibitions Alan was in his element as both players had such illustrious careers to milk the introductions with. He started with Jimmy, 'Ladies and Gentlemen, please put your hands together and welcome the greatest entertainer in snooker today. He is the greatest player never to have won a world championship, but he has the cheekiest smile in London and he is the housewives' choice. Please welcome the man they call the "Whirlwind", the talk of London town, Jimmy the Whirlwind White!' The crowds went wild with delight as Jimmy entered the arena, waving to his many loyal fans. Then Alan had to introduce Alex – and that's when it all started to go wrong. Alan started his introduction, 'Ladies and gentlemen, please give a huge Derby welcome to the man who revolutionised snooker. The man who won the Irish Masters with a broken leg, the man who came from 7–0 down to beat Steve Davis to win the UK Championship, twice world champion and the very man who inspired his opponent Jimmy White when the Whirlwind was just a warm breeze . . .'. Alan was then lost for Alex's name and no matter how much he tried, he just couldn't remember it. So, he thought he'd try again and maybe that would prompt his memory; 'Ladies and gentlemen please welcome to Derby the unforgettable, the unmistakable . . .'. Suddenly, from behind the screen, Higgins said, 'You've even forgotten me f***ing name Hughsey,' which was enough to prompt Alan back to the fore. 'Ladies and gentlemen, the two times world champion, the peoples' champion himself, the one and only Alex Hurricane Higgins!' With that, Alex came out from behind the screen to tumultuous applause from the crowd – or maybe it was a round of applause for Alan Hughes for remembering, at last, the Hurricane's name. Alex has remained a friend of Alan ever since, but rarely lets him forget that incident.

WILLIE WIN IT PARROTT FASHION?

Willie Thorne is a well known gambler, like most snooker players. However, even with his knowledge of the players' habits he doesn't always come out on top with a punt.

Willie Thorne was commentating on a John Parrott match. Now Willie will tell you himself that he often punts huge sums on a bet, be it a horse race or a snooker match, and especially if he has some inside info on the competition. In this particular match, Willie knew from the night before that John Parrott had had his favourite cue stolen. Willie also knew that it was a bad omen for any snooker player to lose his cue. He decided to clean up at the bookies with a big bet of £38,000 for Parrott to lose. Feeling very smug with himself, but trying to hide it, Willie was loving it as John went three down. With Parrott making breaks of less than 50, Willie was very confident of winning the bet and getting himself back on track with his recent losses. Then the play suddenly changed and Parrott was getting on top. Worse still, Willie had to make out he was delighted for the under dog, while secretly wishing he would flunk all his shots. By frame nine, Parrott was 5–4 up and playing much more consistently. Gritting his teeth in the final frame, Willie spoke highly of John's courage in making the best of a bad day. It was one of his worst days gambling but, nevertheless, he had to keep smiling and making out he was pleased for John.

TO PEE OR NOT TO PEE; THAT IS THE QUESTION!

Alex Higgins is well known for taking a pee where and when the feeling takes him. However, it has landed him into trouble on numerous occasions.

A few nights before winning the world championship in 1982, Alex was practising late into the evening after everyone else had gone home. Not being one to break away from his game for a wee, Alex decided to take a leak in a flower pot in the arena. He was seen by a maintenance man who reported him to the WPBSA who always had disciplinary hearings on the morning after the final at Sheffield. After winning the trophy, Alex was ordered to appear before the committee to hear the charge. Ray Reardon, whom Alex had beat to become world champion again, was sitting on the committee that morning. Alex was called into the room in the Grosvenor House Hotel to face the charge. Asked if he had anything to say he replied that he was genuinely sorry. He further promised that in future he would be a champion to be proud of – this obviously went down well with the committee who believed his sincere speech. He was asked to leave the room while they deliberated his punishment. Most members were hopeful that Alex winning the title would make him a nicer person in the future. Shortly afterwards a waiter opened the door and entered with a trolley full of orange juice and champagne for the committee. 'This is with the compliments of Mr Alex Higgins, the new world champion,' the waiter informed them. Feeling rather pleased with themselves and praising his new-found ways, they opened a bottle and were sipping to his health when the door opened again. This time it was Alex holding his daughter Lauren in his arms. 'How long is this going to take?' he demanded in his old manner. The members all looked at each other and knew that nothing was going to change about Alex, but it was nice while it lasted. They told him to go home and they would give him a call later. Two decisions were made that morning: number 1 was that in future no alcohol would be allowed into committee meetings, and the second decision was that Alex was to be fined the maximum for the offence, £1,000. He's often his own worst enemy is Alex.

IT'S NO LAUGHING MATTER, BUT HE HAD ME IN STITCHES . . . AGAIN!

Ken Doherty is nicknamed 'The Darling of Dublin' by his fans, but his family nicknamed him 'The Walking Accident' many years earlier.

Ken Doherty's love of snooker started after an accident he had aged seven, which was later to be the cause of one of his many nicknames. I've already mentioned why Ken is called 'Scarface', but I want to tell you the full story as told to me by Ken himself. As a kid, Ken loved to have adventures and climbing around on roofs was part of it. One day he was climbing on the shed roof when he fell as he tried to jump over the apex. Ken went down fast and hit a dustbin full on. In those days the family had a metal dustbin which all the old folks called an ash can, from the days when they used to empty their fire ashes into them. He hit the lid so hard it sliced his face, and a gash opened up which spurted blood everywhere. His cries of panic and shock, as well as the noise of him hitting the bin, brought his dad out to see what he had done. He took him up in his arms and brought the injured and shocked Ken inside. Still holding him tight he tried to stem the flow of blood, but Ken went into shock. He told me, 'I knew what was happening around me, but I couldn't focus on anything and I seemed to be drifting in some sort of a dream.' He was driven to Baggot Street hospital, but they said that the cut was too deep for them to deal with and they were afraid they would leave him with a big scar. So he was sent over to the children's hospital at Harcourt Street where they were more used to dealing with child injuries. As it turned out, the delay in getting him stitched up caused the tissue around the wound to die and the scar is now quite prominent. However, it doesn't bother him – it has always been a good conversation piece and at school he was left alone by the bullies. He said of the incident, 'I did, however, take it to heart. I was very lucky not to have bled to death, and the experience still haunts me a bit even today. I am constantly reminded of it when I read references to me in articles – they'll often say something like Ken "Scarface" Doherty won such and such a frame or whatever.' That Christmas, Ken got a miniature snooker table for his big pressie, and was hooked on snooker forever, much to the delight of all his fans.

I CAME TO 'BIG IT UP', BUT NOW I'M GIVING UP INSTEAD!

Dennis Taylor was world champion in 1985. Returning to defend his title in 1986 he was another victim of the 'Crucible Curse'. The curse says that no one will win the title twice on the trot.

Like all good champions, Dennis returned full of confidence in 1986 to win the title again, and hoping to beat the curse. It was a short-lived confidence though as he was beaten 10–6 and was out in the first round against Mike Hallett. Never faltering in his sense of humour, Dennis wooed the crowds and put an even bigger smile on Mike's face when he tied a handkerchief around the top of his cue and waved it around like a flag of surrender; what a great loser he truly is with not a bad bone in his body!

DID YOU HEAR THE ONE ABOUT THE SNOOKER PLAYER WHO . . . ?

In an exhibition match there is always plenty of banter and humour between the audience and the players. However, sometimes they can get a bit carried away. At one such exhibition Ray Reardon and John Pulman went the whole hog.

I heard this story when I was invited to the UK Championships at Wembley by Jimmy White in 2006. The story is well known in snooker circles. One night,

John Pulman and Ray Reardon were booked to play an exhibition. The hall was packed and the two players had been practicing in the main arena before the doors opened. John suggested to Ray that they go the extra mile, and really entertain the crowds with plenty of banter and a few anecdotes. One of the things that all the players and a few of the managers are really good at is impersonating Alex Higgins, so at these matches, when an Alex story is told, the accent and facial mannerisms are rife.

They entered the arena to the usual introductions and started their first frame, John won the toss so he decided to have first break. He hit the reds but failed to pot any. However, he did set some shots up for Ray. Ray stepped up and, in true snooker style worthy of a champion player, he scored a 147 to the delight of the crowd and John. John then stood up and took the microphone, 'Ladies and gentlemen you have just witnessed a true artist of the baize, and how can I possibly follow that?' John then proceeded to put his cue away in the case, while Ray and the crowd looked on in sheer amazement. Ray and the audience then waited for the punchline. He continued, 'If people want to watch great snooker then you folks have just seen the perfect frame from Ray. However, if it's entertainment you want then I'm your man.' Ray sat down while John then entertained the whole arena with an array of great stories, which lasted for 2 hours and 15 minutes.

One of the stories he told was about the time Alex Higgins was nearly drowned in Hong Kong Harbour. It was during the Hong Kong Open when some of the players had a day off. A local businessman who was a fan invited the boys onto his yacht for a day of entertainment, fishing and, if they were brave enough, a little swim. The yacht went about a mile offshore and the drink was flowing, as was the banter. Willie Thorne was looking at the ocean and remarked that it looked calm and clean enough to swim in. The host invited them to avail themselves of the yacht's towels and have a dip. Without waiting for another hint, Willie and most of the boys stripped off and jumped in, all except Alex. Alex was well known to have a fear of water – he never learned to swim. However, Alex hates being left out of a good time and was itching to join them. In true Higgy style he asked a crew member if he could put him in a lifeboat and lower him down onto the water. The chap went away and came back with a large rubber ring shaped like a swan, and Higgy's face lit up at the prospect of joining in the fun. He stripped down to his pants and carefully climbed down the ladder that hung over the side. Now Alex hadn't quite thought this one out (as usual) and as he lowered himself into the swan (which was on the water already) he began to feel the fear. Looking up at the crew member, Alex made him promise that he wouldn't let go of the rope that the swan was attached to, which was about 20-odd feet long. Alex was sitting on the swan with his legs dangling over the sides and hanging onto the neck for dear life. He then paddled with his feet as the fear seemed to leave him.

What no one had seen was that a speedboat had gone past the yacht about a quarter of a mile away, and by the time Alex was at the full end of the rope, the wash from the boat hit the side and bounced back towards him. Alex lost his balance as the swan tipped to one side and dipped his head down towards the water, but he didn't fall off. Instead he got the rope caught around his neck, and now the wash was taking him away from the yacht and tightening the rope – Alex thought he was about to peg it. Onboard the yacht watching all this was Joe Johnson and his manager Wally Springett, neither of whom were partial to swimming that day. Wally looked at Joe as if to say, 'Well go on then, save him!' But Joe had no intention of going over the side – he feared that a shark would be attracted by all the splashing and he didn't want to end up as its dinner. Joe did, however, manage to grab the rope and pull Alex towards the larger stairs of the yacht, and although Alex was purple and nearly unconscious, he pulled him up and helped him to the deck. Joe feared Higgy was going to clock him one, but Alex just hugged him and thanked him for saving his life. As he took a glass of vodka and orange, he shook Joe's hand and said, 'You've saved my life, babe, I'll always be in your debt.'

CUED UP AND CLUED UP!

Many players rely on their favourite cues to help them win matches. If they lose them or they get damaged then it can seriously deflate their confidence.

Jimmy White is not so fanatical about his cue as say Steve Davis is. Steve is so protective of his cue that only about three people are allowed to even touch it. If Steve is disturbed during a practice session he won't leave his cue on the table; he will pack it away in its case.

Alex Higgins is the master of cue care and knows a cue better than most players. It may be because he was good with his hands at school and especially liked woodwork. Jimmy has given away some of his cues to friends, but he has also received cues from Higgy. Jimmy once gave his best mate, Peewee, the cue that he won the World Amateur title with in 1980. Peewee was ecstatic at owning such a piece of history and guarded it with pride. However, his car was stolen and in the boot was the cue. Although he eventually got the car back, the cue disappeared, and he never dared to admit it to Jimmy. Some months later, a bloke knocked on Jimmy's door and returned the cue – he knew it was his as it had his name on it. Feeling peeved that Peewee hadn't told him about the loss, he then gave it to a young disabled fan whom he met at an exhibition. When Peewee found out, he was so upset he refused to speak to Jimmy for ages. When Peewee was later told that Jimmy had given his cue to the lad, he was so taken with the gesture that he made it up with him.

TALK ABOUT ONE BORN EVERY MINUTE!

Jimmy Caras was one of America's most prolific players of billiards. He claimed just before his death in December 2002 at the age of ninety-three, that he had been playing the game for eighty-seven years. His father was a Greek immigrant who owned a billiards bar in New York.

He repeatedly represented the Brunswick company at exhibitions and had a lifetime of stories to tell. Here are a few rarely known ones.

'I was just thirteen and already a good player, I came home from school one day and was looking forward to putting my feet up and having some lemonade. As I came into the bar to go upstairs my dad was standing at the billiard table with another man, he was holding a cue and smiling. Dad called me over and introduced me as his son, the man shook my hand. Dad said he had lined up a match for me, the best of five. As the man racked up the balls dad announced to the bar that he was putting up $100 for me to play the man. As I walked over to the cash register to put my books behind the bar, the drawer was open and I peeked inside to see only $35 in there. Dad came over and I said to him, 'What if I lose, Pa?' He just looked at me and, smiling through his moustache, he shrugged his shoulders and said, 'You won't son.' That is why I never suffer from pressure when I am playing in a tight match; it was like being taught to swim by your dad throwing you in the river and shouting, 'Now get out of that!'

In his sixties Caras was visiting an old friend who owned a billiards bar in New Jersey. When he arrived the friend was at the wholesalers so he sat at the bar and had a beer. After a few minutes a teenage boy came in and looked around. Spotting this old man at the bar he walked up to him and struck up a conversation about billiards. Jimmy asked him how well he played, but never let on who he was.

'I'm the best player in town mister; I'll play you a buck a game to prove it.' Jimmy raised his eyebrows in amazement at the youngster's belief in himself; maybe he was seeing himself at that age.

'Don't worry sir, I'll go easy on you, I promise,' said the young man and then he racked up the table. Jimmy wiped the floor with him by winning 18 games on the trot. As the last ball dropped into the pocket, the teenager's face was a picture to see – he had just lost $18 and was now broke. Jimmy picked up the money and gave it back to him with a smile.

'Why did you pick on me?' he asked the teenager. He replied, 'Well sir, you looked like a sucker.' Which just goes to prove that you can never judge a player by looks alone!

LOCK THE DOORS, CALL THE COPS, WE'RE ALL GETTING 'STONED'

Jimmy White was in Dublin with his manager Kevin Kelly and they opted to stay a day longer as rocker Ronnie Wood was also in town and decided they needed a night out. They started at around 3 o'clock in the afternoon in Grafton Street. As they all knew the owner of the Bruxelles Bar, they soon ended up there. The bar was in full swing with a local Irish band playing to the tourists, and the odd street trader who dropped in every now and then. No one took much notice until one of the band saw and recognised the famous pair.

'Jeeesus, will yer look der? It's only Ronnie Wood and the Whirlwind . . . how'r yer fellas?', he exclaimed. The three of them raised their glasses and carried on. After a few times of trying to get Ronnie to join the band, he relented and was handed a guitar as he went over to the corner of the bar. Within minutes their table was full of complimentary drinks, and the word went round that the Rolling Stone was playing a gig in the bar. After a few numbers Ronnie was well into the session and the bar staff were locking the doors to stop the bar overcrowding. Jimmy was clapping and singing along to the band as the crowds outside started building up. The cops were called by the Westbury Hotel as the mob was blocking the narrow street and the entrance to the hotel. A riot nearly broke out as the cops turned up in droves to disperse the crowds. Ronnie just carried on totally oblivious of the goings on outside. When they read the next day's papers they couldn't believe they had caused so much trouble, innocently. Ronnie had to promise the Dublin Gardai to never play for nothing again. They ended the night in the Piano Bar of Lillie's Bordello just a three-minute walk from the Bruxelles, where Ronnie played the piano and Jimmy sang along to his duets with the resident singer.

HE'S A CELEBRITY . . . GET ME OUT OF HERE!

One of the earliest anecdotes in billiards and snooker history involves the nineteenth-century billiards champion John Roberts. In 1885 he was introduced to the game snooker while on a visit to India. He was already a well-known champion billiards player and it is generally believed that he was actually responsible for introducing snooker to the billiards players of England. He wasn't a real world champion as such, just a great player at a time when there were no world championship competitions. One of the many anecdotes about him involves a challenge one day in a billiards room in India. He was always immaculately dressed and always looked the gentleman he was. As he came into the room he was approached by a hustler, who asked Roberts if he fancied a game with a side bet.

'I'll give you a 40 start,' he said, then continued, 'the winner will be the first to get 100 points.' Roberts was quite amused and, being the gentleman he was, he decided to be honest and handed the man his card. The card read 'John Roberts Jr Billiards Champion'. Thinking that would be the end of the matter, he smiled and went to walk on. The challenger read the card and as Roberts walked off he called him back and said, 'Ah! In that case I'll make it a 20 points start.' Roberts beat him and won the bet, but the man said it was worth it for the lesson he had had from a real champion. John Roberts called himself Jr because his father John was also a champion of the game. Roberts Jr went onto to be an influence along with William Cook, another early champion, in setting out the rules for the game for the first Billiards Association.

'FATS' LIFE

Rudolf Walter Wanderone was a famous billiards player in America. Born in 1913 he went on to become the most recognisable player in the world. In 1959 Walter

Trevis wrote a book about billiards called *The Hustler*, in which he calls his hero Minnesota Fats. Wanderone was well known on the billiards hall circuit by a series of similar nicknames, which he got from his large frame, allegedly acquired from his love of Wimpy burgers. Now Wanderone was a known chancer and infamous hustler, who never missed a trick. He threatened to sue Trevis, alleging that the book was based on his career as a champion player. At that time he was known as 'New York Fats', but had also been called 'Chicago Fats' and 'Broadway Fats' when it suited him. He was in fact an entertainer who used to play billiards in between gigs to earn a living. In 1961 *The Hustler* was made into a film starring Paul Newman and in the film, Newman plays against a character named 'Minnesota Fats'. At the time Wanderone was still known as 'New York Fats'. A passing remark by world champion Willie Mosconi, who was technical advisor on the film, gave Wanderone the idea to sue Trevis, although he actually never did, and change his name again to the fictitious 'Minnesota Fats'. He went onto play himself as the character of 'Minnesota Fats' in the film *The Player*, made in 1970. He promoted the movie as the lead actor and appeared on TV and billboards all over the country. He became a huge world-famous entertainer and was the man who made billiards, and subsequently snooker, a sport with entertaining characters. He appeared on all sorts of shows from *What's my Line?* to the *David Frost Show*, and moved in the same circles as Hollywood film stars. This man made himself world-famous out of that chance remark by Willie Mosconi, and never looked back. Muhammad Ali taking place, so the pair, dragging the dog, went to have a nose at the entrance to the church. Peering through the crack in the door they watched the bride and groom turn and walk up the aisle. As they turned they saw the dog crouched and noticed, mainly by the smell at first, that he had relieved himself on the floor. Quickly turning and legging it out of the church, with the poor dog still relieving itself, they raced off in embarrassment. As they went through the gates they could hear the screams and shouts as the bride and groom ventured into the 'message' left by the dog. Sadly, the dog was so ill that they had to have him put down, and Alex never bought another greyhound or, incidentally, learned to drive.

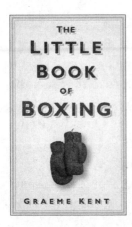

THE LITTLE BOOK OF BOXING
Graeme Kent
ISBN 978 0 7524 5253 1

An unrivalled feast of the sport's drama, excitement and ribaldry, *The Little Book of Boxing* is a must-have for any fight fan. The champs, the chumps, the thrills, spills and fixes, the heroes and villains – they are all here!

THE LITTLE BOOK OF LONDON
David Long
ISBN 978 0 7509 4800 5

The Little Book of London is a funny, fast-paced compendium of frivolous, fantastic and simply strange information which no-one will want to be without. With its wacky facts and anecdotes, it is essential reading for visitors and locals alike.

**Visit our website and discover thousands
of other History Press books.**

www.thehistorypress.co.uk

always said he based his showbiz persona on a wrestler name 'Gorgeous George', who was always saying how handsome he was. Wanderone met him once and used to insist after that meeting that Ali really based his persona on him.

I TOLD THE DOG TO 'SIT', HONEST!

Alex Higgins is well known for his love of betting – horses, dogs or flies walking up a wall, it doesn't matter. Like all gamblers Alex always fancied himself as a trainer; he was a trainee jockey after leaving school, but gave it up after some incidents with a horse who didn't like him. When Alex became famous as a snooker player he often got fans to offer to drive him to the next match. He was in the Republic of Ireland in the 1970s and after a match he was driven to the home of a fan. The fan was a breeder of greyhounds and Alex was fascinated to hear all about it. After a few drinks and a lot of banter, Alex left the house with a greyhound in tow. He returned to Belfast with the dog, but didn't fancy looking after it himself as he was too busy playing snooker for a living. So, sister Jean was recruited to look after the dog and they soon found out that it couldn't win a raffle if it had all the tickets – let alone a race. The next day Jean took the dog for a walk – this was after she cleaned up the mess that the poor animal had made after consuming some home-made stew the night before. Meeting a friend, they walked together around the streets until they passed the church. Jean heard the bells ringing and said that a wedding must be